INTO THE UNIVERSE

EXTRATERRESTRIAL ACTIVITIES

The Collected Works
of Gregge Tiffen

P Systems & Associates, Publishers
La Jolla, California

Copyright 2010
By
G-Systems International

All Rights Reserved

———————

ISBN: 978-0-9842552-1-4

P Systems & Associates, Publishers
La Jolla, California

Into the Universe: Extraterrestrial Activities
Published by P Systems & Associates
P.O. Box 12754
La Jolla, CA 92039
www.P-SystemsInc.com

While we appreciate your enthusiasm for sharing our work, please remind yourself of what you know about copyrighted information. Here's a refresher: All rights Reserved. No parts of this publication may be reproduced, stored in or introduced into a retrieval system, or transmitted, in any form or by any means (electronic, mechanical, photocopying, recording or otherwise), without the prior written consent. The scanning, uploading, and distribution of this book via the Internet or by any other means without the permission of G-Systems International is illegal and punishable by law. Your support of these rights is appreciated. Thank you.

To contact G-Systems International, visit www.g-systems.com, email Bonnie@g-systems.com, or call 1-972-447-9092.

For general information about other publications, visit our web site www.P-SystemsInc.com or call our toll free number 1.888.658.0668.

Transcribed and written by Patrece Powers
Graphic Design: Isla Cordelae
Editorial assistance: Cindy Reinhardt
                       Isla Cordelae
                       Renne Evans

Printed in the United States of America
on recycled paper (80% post consumer)

To extraterrestrial visitors

Whose explorations bring them
to our solar system and onto Planet Earth.
May the information gathered provide them
with the worthwhile knowledge they are seeking.

These Works of mysticism update that which would otherwise be left behind.

--Gregge Tiffen

Contents

Introduction: The Collected Works 1

Planet Earth: A Research Laboratory 3

Extraterrestrial Activities 9

  1. Types of Extraterrestrial Visitors 13
  2. Technological Considerations 15
  3. Sustenance Systems 17
  4. Basic Reasons for Spaceship Missions 19
  5. Base Colonization 23
  6. Identifying Characteristics 25
  7. Command Structure 27
  8. Time Warp 32
  9. Sunspots 35
  10. Transmitting Stations 36
  11. Negative Effects 42
  12. Ship Construction 44
  13. Propulsion Systems 44
  14. Ship Size 48
  15. Ship's Complement 49
  16. Transfer of Information 51
  17. Navigational Systems 52
  18. Safety Precaution 54
  19. Life Support Systems 56
  20. Communication with Planet Earth 57
  21. Landing Procedures 59
  22. Disease Regression 60
  23. Spacecraft Encounters 62
  24. Debriefing 64

Conclusion: Macrocosmic and Microcosmic Principles 67

Introduction
The Collected Works

The Collected Works is a compilation of presentations from Gregge Tiffen's lectures and teachings to which the reader can return beneficially time and time again. Gregge had little time to write due to the sheer magnitude of teaching and lecturing activities that increased year-by-year throughout more than five decades of his work in the field of meta-energy. In addition to his business consultations and lectures, his days were spent meeting the needs of people who sought guidance for personal and professional concerns.

He consistently refused requests to form an organization of any kind in order to insure that his unique training in mysticism, including the Universal Laws of Independence and Individuality, would find the proper audience. He felt certain that such teachings must not be frame-worked within organizations. By their very design, organizations develop a hierarchy of personalities that regrettably destroy the atmosphere necessary for the purity required to learn and to teach, to lead and to follow.

The style and presentation of materials published in this series of The Collected Works are Gregge's unaltered spoken words. There is very little editorial license in order to maintain the clarity of precision that identifies how he was taught and, as a result, how he taught. The timeless nature of knowledge precludes indicating dates and locations of his teachings. In this way, we are able to support and promote the integrity of Gregge's life-long dedication to up-date and correct misinterpretations of ancient wisdoms.

Since all lectures were delivered to an audience familiar with Gregge's mystical training and orientation, we suggest those who are unacquainted with those principles familiarize themselves by reading his highly acclaimed book: *Life in the World Hereafter, The Journey Continues.* It is truly an adventure you won't want to miss. Don't leave earth without it!

Part I
Planet Earth-A Research Laboratory

> *Planet Earth provides a window*
> *for extraterrestrial test programs.*
> ---GT

As time goes on, I think we are going to have more and more extraterrestrial visitors. However, after dealing with the pressures of everyday events and survival issues, it is very hard for us to give much, if any, attention to our part in what this means in the Universal scheme of things. That is a very unfortunate situation. Disinterest leaves a person in the position of just taking what comes along without any basic functional and fundamental know-how. Nevertheless, the time has definitely come for us to include awareness of our part in the Grand Design and the affect extraterrestrial activity has on our galaxy, our solar system, and on our planet – Earth.

A necessary perspective is accomplished when we understand Universal Laws. Everything, without exception, has a function and a natural progression. Galaxies consist of a combination of an undetermined number of stars without any set size, density, or energy output. And every solar system within the trillions of galaxies throughout the one Universe has definitive characteristics. In other words, there can be billions of stars within one galaxy, and each of those stars has a different characteristic in support of the galaxial function.

The characteristic of our solar system, including Planet Earth as a basic value star laboratory, is that it serves as a major training and proving ground for extraterrestrial's research. It is the function of each and every celestial body within our solar system to work within this basic concept of research.

On our planet, we have three basic functions, each of which has a significant identifiable vibratory rate. The functions are distinguished by the input and output of energy that we call spiritual, mental, and physical functions. Although the energies overlap, they are not similar in frequency rates. Your arrival here has been allowed because of your capabilities developed over an infinite amount of time. You need to be aware that you are at one of the highest conceivable levels of existence due to your ability to consistently adjust to the three energetic functions: the spiritual, the mental, and the physical. This indicates enormous evolution on the part of every inhabitant.

None of us is single-minded with single capabilities, and it is this multiplicity of being able to adjust that gives us capabilities of long range possibilities. However, I do not want to infer that this is not difficult. It is! Everything is a test event within our solar system, and the results of research occur in the culmination of evaluation for some test program somewhere. It is important to remember that each of us is a contributor to a test unit in a research laboratory that includes this planet, this solar system, and this galaxy.

There are unstable incoming energy levels that penetrate the earth. Without those energies we would not have the variables needed, and we absorb those energies as situations in order to find a solution. This is a tough job.

You might be asking yourself if extraterrestrials are so advanced and intelligent, why they would bother to stop off here. Well, we have basic functional know-how that they don't have within the physical, mental, and spiritual frequencies. Technically, this allows us to operate with broad range decision-making capabilities that serve them for evaluation purposes.

In a more mundane sense, we are also aware of testing programs taking place. We set up a vibratory pattern (something that works), and then we change it in order to learn from our own involvement. Individually that means that you are testing your ability to understand yourself, your ability to get along with other people, and your ability to put definitive effort into the world to make something out of your efforts – one test after another. Your ability to get things that satisfy and fulfill you is a constant re-balancing of energy.

How many times have you started over? How many times have you turned around and gone in a different direction? How many times have you heard someone say, "This didn't work out, but I have found another way that is even better"? All of these examples are proof of a constant testing program, albeit at the very smallest level within the concept of the whole test unit activity. Re-balancing is a major portion of the evaluation process.

Humanity, as a mass unit, produces a very unique experience. We call those experiences events. All events are produced by the mass. I meet you. Technically speaking, that is an event. What brought me to that point and what brought you to that point of meeting is a whole conglomerate of activity. How is it that I was right there when you needed me, and you were right there when I needed you? Is that by design? What design? Your design? My design? Yes, but his, hers, theirs, ours is a design as a constant conglomerate of activity.

Take the election of a president for an example. When the person gets elected, we are looking at a mass function of a test unit coming to the point of culmination. We are also looking at a point of culmination of a test program that was contributed to by a large mass of people, either directly or indirectly. What we have is a series of these test events that come to some point of evaluation. Everyone who does an evaluation is evaluating a test program. First we have something set up, and then we completely wipe it out and start over. You have got to know that the extraterrestrials view this with amazement. This is totally fascinating to them. We like to think that our intent is to make all the necessary adjustments and changes in order to operate as smoothly as possible. However, the result of our action, as an evaluation process, is most often criticism, which most of us have mastered very well!

An evaluation of any test event takes into consideration what went right or wrong. <u>The</u> Question: Did you learn anything you could personally use about yourself from the event? Since all events pertain to you personally, the idea is to evaluate and learn from events. Your existence is growth for you; although, as a participant, you also contribute as a part of a major test unit on the planet. What are <u>you</u> trying to test?

Earth is a major star laboratory within the basic value of our whole solar system that serves as a major test area. Within the spiritual, mental, and physical frequency factors, we have a broad range of conditions that the extraterrestrials don't have. Because we are physical, the *'viewers'* can see us in more than nebulous forms. This makes us a valuable laboratory for intense research that offers a magnitude of test activities to weigh and balance results.

Pregnancy, childbirth, infancy, old age, and regeneration are all astounding to them. With cellular regeneration, how can a body only be seven years old at any one time and still grow old? How can a physical body function in so many modes? Why do some people have blue eyes, and other people have brown eyes? How is it that we can breathe air filled with smog and still survive? Or, can we? How can we operate from sub-zero to one-hundred-and-ten-degree temperatures? Extraterrestrials from other galaxies have to operate on a steady temperature basis.

For centuries we used coal and wood as a natural resource. Now we are in the process of changing to a whole new concept of energy. This change of energy use on our planet is just one obvious example of how we are constantly readjusting. This is the kind of adaptability wanted in outer space. The only problem is that you don't think any of this is very important to you. It is very important as you go along in life that you are aware of the testing program. That is true awareness.

Someday, we will go elsewhere from this intense, vital laboratory that we currently call home. However, before we leave here we will have the key to unifying the distinct spiritual, mental, and physical energy levels into one unit. Until then, and while you participate in this on-going test program, may you have a greater awareness and appreciation of your part in the magnificent Design.

The Universe is not testing you.
You test you as part of a test unit.

Part II
Extraterrestrial Activities

> *I would venture to say that there are a lot of people who have had very positive contacts and have never said a word about them.*
> --GT

The day has come for people to understand that we have not only been pioneers about life in outer space but also about the ability of that life to transport itself and communicate with us.

Be assured, the source of this material is heavily dependent upon my own personal experiences. I have no idea if this information is going to be (or ever will be) of any use to you. I have no idea if any of you will ever personally see one of these *'individuals'*, or if you will ever personally get a ride on a spacecraft. Neither do I know if you will ever even be involved on the fringes. On the other hand, the possibility is rising fast that you will have direct contact in one way or another. In 1969 the odds were in the magnitude of seventy-five-billion-to-one. Those odds are dropping faster everyday, primarily because by 1974 we were already getting an increase in saucer activity. That will continue. The odds of an encounter increase out in areas such as Arizona, northern California at Tahoe, and in New Mexico. The Great Lakes are definitely being used because it is a large water mass even though it is locked in by land. Also, there is a great deal of activity off Point Sur, south of Carmel, California, at Little Sur. This is due to the ability to hide the ships in the atmospheric conditions found there.

10. Into the Universe

I don't honestly think we can possibly exclude the idea from our awareness that we do have entities from our galaxy and other galaxies who have made the trip. Actually, there is a great amount of evidence that has piled up over the years from valid investigators that indicate more than just the possibility of extraterrestrial activity. Such validation has been completely ignored by a society that refuses to believe in anything they don't understand. This is particularly true with anything considered incredulous.

At this particular time (1974), the government has transferred what they consider a 'problem' from the Air Force to NASA. They say this will downgrade the subject. Nevertheless, reports continue to leak out from both pilots and the government that confirm validation in some areas of space travel and communication.

If you go back into early historical writings, you will discover a great deal of what was apparently extraterrestrial activity and visitations. Those writings appeared in Chinese manuscripts some five thousand years ago. They indicate the presence of certain teaching capabilities found in ancient civilizations in which there is no idea how that knowledge got there through any labor of humans. Such questions are a long way from being answered, and it will probably be decades before we have amassed information, in one form or another, to finally bring us to the awareness of this highly voluble subject. It does not seem possible or proper at this fragile and susceptible time in history.

I can understand if people think this is ridiculous, but I am not trying to convince anyone of anything. My attitude about this is what I know from experience. This is what I know can happen, this is what I know will happen, and this is what I know is happening.

My first encounter with these *individuals* occurred not long before I got into this work. It was a negative type incident that upset me to such an extent that it remains with me to this day as one of the most vivid things that ever happened in my life. The positive incident that happened a year-and-a-half to two years later was an experience of a completely different nature. As we go along, I will bring out some of the aspects of those two incidents.

Over a period of years, my contact with different types of extraterrestrial *individuals* has been fairly frequent, sometimes as astral trips and mostly as a means of information gathering. As I have already indicated, I am basing what I tell you on that background of knowledge and association. For the benefit of everyone, I must add that I have no way of validating this information for you. I am turning it out to you more as a premise of what I know to be true until you have your own experience at some later time. As long as you do not have the experience, we may always have a quarrel about it. I am not in any position to argue my point yea or nay.

I have appeared on radio shows a couple of times regarding these topics of discussion. As always, there were callers who called in to say they believed and those who told the announcer to get that nut off the air. They thought it was ridiculous. When you get into this kind of area, it is very hard to substantiate any of the information from shared experiences, let alone, find an appropriate and accurate language.

The problem of semantics applies to mysticism itself. We definitely do not have any terms that fit into our dictionary for inter-galaxial transportation and communication. It is not just their language, whatever that might be, that makes accurate communication difficult. Just trying to identify certain aspects is also very difficult. For example, they use certain metals and propulsion systems that we have absolutely no terminology for, nor do we have any semantics in terms of their time-distance-speed ratio. In other words, we cannot talk to them in terms of time, distance, or speed because they operate on a totally different level. As I go along, you will find certain types of extraterrestrials use different descriptive terminology.

I am translating as much of this as I can into known terms. Initially, you need to recognize that this approach leaves a great deal to be desired. It is highly questionable whether I am even coming close to giving you a purely accurate description by using certain terms. Since we don't have a common denominator, there is no way I can give you an accurate description of the amount of energy turned out by the types of propulsion systems they use. Where we might harness nuclear power, they tend (in some cases) to harness light power. They also tend to harness certain types of energy, the likes of which are unfamiliar to us.

Look at how many years we have been dealing with electricity. Let's go back to Benjamin Franklin and the pipeline incident. Two hundred years later we are just now learning about electricity as it pertains to semi-conductors and micro-miniature electronics. We have not even begun to scratch the surface. If we are at that elementary state of the art, consider what we run into when we start talking about extraterrestrials who have amassed knowledge twenty times greater than ours. They are using materials and energy that are super-electrical, super-light forces, super atomic forces; all of which we have not even begun to discover, or understand, or achieve in our scientific capacities. That truly remains a tremendous problem in communication. I come to an absolute dead end when I try to translate what they would be willing to pass on to us because knowledge is passed on to me in a non-verbal category. It is easy for me to understand them, but I am trying to keep the knowledge within that context in order to pass the essence along to you on a level that is understandable.

As you go along, you need to give yourself plenty of time to accept this material.

Types of Extraterrestrials

We basically have four types of extraterrestrial visitors. For the sake of simplicity, I have identified them as Type A, Type B, Type C, and Type D. Here again, I have taken my own literary license to identify them as I see fit. This has no direct meaning to the way they identify themselves.

Type A and Type B are the intra-galaxial types that we have the most chance of seeing, and they are the ones that are most often ignored. Type A is intra-galaxial positive. These are *individuals* who come here from within our galaxy. They are indicated as intra-galaxial positive because their activity relationship is on a positive base form. That is, they have positive reasons for making the trip and positive reasons for dealing with us in a certain way.

Type B is intra-galaxial negative. This is the type I had for my first encounter. They are considerably dangerous for any number of reasons. You see, we just assume that if we have extraterrestrial visitors who have the ability to bring a spacecraft from X thousand number of miles away that they have a superior intelligence, and that they have a spiritual attitude regarding spiritual humanitarian efforts. This is simply not true. You need to understand that technology does not establish a criterion for spirituality. In many cases, advanced technology can do just the opposite.

It can tend to make the *individuals* very overbearing and allow them to feel that their power is indestructible. They think they can use their technological skills with impunity when, where, and how they so desire. They come from their own star system that is not the same Star Base as Type A-positive, and they do have, in some cases, nefarious reasons and means for arriving. They also have their limitations. In effect, somewhere in the magnitude of eighty to ninety percent of all extraterrestrial visitors are Type A (intra-galaxial positive), and Type B (intra-galaxial negative).

I do not know how to share this without sounding overly dramatic, but the Type B-negative group that I got involved in during my first encounter had a high technological capability with electrical charge currents that almost electrocuted me. The electrical charge so burned the consciousness and sight that it literally took me weeks to recover. To this day, I have never forgotten the incident. It is in my recall as if it happened yesterday. That leads me to believe that there is a very strong residue that can remain for a long period of time as a result of such an incident.

Type C is inter-galaxial. These are the types whose home base is not within this galaxy. I generally categorize them in a more positive mode because I have never had an incident with them that was negative, but I am sure that somewhere along the line they must have negative polarities.

Type D is also inter-galaxial. These are types who are of *very* high technological advancement coming out of super galaxies. They tend to be as advanced in a mystical, humanitarian sense as we might like to think of those qualities in the cosmic visitors who feel benevolent. Any one of these four identifiable groups (or a combination of them) would be in and around the solar system at any given time. This brings up the point that the target of these visitations is not generally Planet Earth, per se. Earth is a very small planet, and we are not terribly important in the whole scheme of things even though we like to think we are. In most cases, if we are talking about <u>inter</u>-galaxial visitors, their choice of arrival has to do with their choice of the solar system not the choice of a planet. They are not really looking for Earth, Mars, or Venus. They are looking for the solar system as part of their investigation. In a way, it is as if you were trying to discover a whole new continent across the sea, and you came across an island. You would say, "This is not the continent I was looking for. It is an island, but isn't it nice. Let's stop off here, and we will get some water then be on our way." You might discover some exciting things there, but that is really not what you are headed for nor do you intend to stay very long.

Type C and Type D, <u>inter</u>-galaxial cosmic types, tend to be using the galaxy as their target area. Their sojourn through our area of contact just happens to be as fleeting as if the President of the United States was riding down Pennsylvania Avenue waving to all the people. There are rare cases where earth has been the target for the cosmic, <u>inter</u>-galaxial Type C and Type D. That is okay. Type A and Type B gives us plenty to try to understand for quite some time.

Technological Considerations

We are as involved with the variance of technology with extraterrestrial visitors as we are with technology on this planet alone. Think of how many types of sciences we have and how many types of scientific minds we have working. It really boggles the mind to consider the hundreds of thousands of different types of work and things we get involved in, yet we make the mistake of compiling all galaxial visitors into one category. We assume that they are all technologically perfect. We also assume that along with their technology they have a broad range of intelligence. This is also not true. Sometimes the technology is very high, but they are dummies and very dangerous dummies in the sense of not having (what we call) a humanitarian sense. There are a lot of times that their technology tends to go awry and gets away from them.

Let's consider the situation where we establish a space station. If something goes awry, we are going to lose it and it would burn up. In such a case, we are faced with a situation where we had the technology to launch it, but we didn't have the technology to keep it up and maintain it. In some cases, extraterrestrials have the knowledge to put the spacecraft together, but they do not have the knowledge to get from point A to point B. They don't have the knowledge to keep the spacecraft from cracking up. They might also have the knowledge to get from point A to point B, but then they don't have the knowledge to keep from damaging point B when they don't want to damage it.

It is a horrible error on our part to assume all extraterrestrials are categorized in a typical ivory tower, and that they are untouchable so everything is going to work out fine. That is not true. Many of them are and many of them are not. We fail to encompass a degree of discernment and awareness that technology does not necessarily lead to spirituality. We must be prepared for areas of variation on a scale running from top to bottom.

In the Hollywood sense, we have categorized and surrounded these visitors with a certain amount of danger and animosity. Horrible things could be present if they arrived without having the controls they were supposed to have. In some cases, they don't have the aesthetic ideals we would like them to have. Therefore, it isn't always the case that we are here to greet them with open arms.

People often say to me that they would like to see an extraterrestrial or that they would like to go on a space ship. Unless you specify a certain type and get that type, you are going to be shocked right out of your boots. It could turn out to be a trip that is no fun at all!

Sustenance Systems

Before we get into the metals and the propulsion guidance systems, you need to recognize that the construction of the *individuals* involved on the journeys is not necessarily physical. Most often we fail to realize that whether the *individuals* are physical or not, they must have life support systems. This is no different than it would be for any astronaut we send into space who requires a life support system that provides oxygen and some kind of food. Both inter-galaxial and intra-galaxial visitors also need life support systems. This is one of the reasons we don't have them running around the streets by the tens of dozens. They cannot do this without their appropriate life support systems to nourish them and keep them alive. You may have already realized that much of their limitation in terms of travel time and travel distance for their mission is related to the quality of those life support systems.

It is important for you to learn to think in the proper categories. It has been too common, and for too long, to assume that these extraterrestrial *individuals* do not eat and do not sleep. We have assumed that they get on their spaceship, someone pushes the button, and off they go a few hundred light years from their Star Base. The assumption has been that they don't need anything. Nothing is further from the truth. Extensive preparations have to be made especially as they pertain to life support systems.

It continues to amaze me that during the periods of *Star Trek* entertainment, no one gave any lip service or any thought to life support systems. The programs showed all extraterrestrials looking pretty healthy to me, and I always wondered what they were eating. Were we supposed to assume that there was something really unusual that they are not telling us? This should not be played down in the movies and television programs! I do not know of any celestial visitors that do not require preparation for a certain level of sustenance to take care of them.

It doesn't make any difference if any of these types are in a physical body or not. They still experience a time warp situation that plays havoc with energy and consciousness. I will discuss this further as we go along. When you are in a time warp situation in a spacecraft, you are going X times the speed of light. You are going 5.8 trillion miles per hour. Cosmic Type C and Type D ships can do this, and it creates an enormous problem on the *individuals* who are encapsulated inside the vehicle. Of course this is going to affect them. If it didn't affect them, what would prevent them from becoming the Gods and Giants of the Universe? They would be able to take over anything and everything. If you are not affected by traveling 5.8 trillion miles an hour, what difference would it make where you go in whatever galaxy? It's illogical to think there would not be an effect upon the extraterrestrial *individuals* in both sustenance and life support systems whatever their form. Otherwise, we would have hundreds arriving in the solar system everyday, and there are just not that many. Also, it is not that easy for them to move around down here.

We are microcosmic in our ways. We are a bunch of cells held together in a body form operated by consciousness. They are also energy forms held together by consciousness but not necessarily in a body. However, they do have an energy form of a microcosmic nature that has to be held together. It also undergoes transport requirements.

Basic Reasons for Spaceship Missions

At this point, we need to consider the causes for each Type (A, B, C, and D) to make a trip. What sends them out from their home star base,wherever that may be, to go out into the galaxies? Actually, there are five very basic reasons, most of which apply to what we do in terms of our own space programs.

Exploration is the biggest reason that sends forth a spacecraft. We like to think that man has curiosity from the need to know; but you must understand that it is a natural function of intelligence in the Universe to have the need to know, the need to explore, and the need to find out. This is not just for knowledge in space, but it *is* to find out what is "out there". I don't know why we would think that we are the only living things in the Universe. Why would it be that we would want to climb mountains and nobody else would want to climb mountains? The further you can travel in terms of trillions of miles, the more serious you become about what is beyond that point. If we could go to Mars or Jupiter, that would spur us on to go further and further. Once we found out what was there and absorbed that knowledge, we would jump off from that point to go out further and still further. Therefore, exploration is the prime reason for their movement, just as it is ours.

Measurement is the second reason for movement out. If you are looking for the constituent of knowledge, it is measurement. There is an interesting system of weights and balances within the Universe. In the same regard that we tend to want to study the moon in order to understand the origins of the earth, extraterrestrials also have a need to take measurements in order to understand what is going on in their star systems. You see, in order for the Universe to stay infinite, it will never allow us to see both ends of the polarities simultaneously. It's impossible. You will never be able to have plus and minus at exactly the same time. You can have plus and then you go search for minus. While you are looking for minus, plus has moved. When you find minus, you go back and look for plus and minus has moved.

Basically, that is what we do when we learn. We measure. We measure against standards that someone else has established or standards we have established. If we have established them, they are known standards. If someone else established them, they are unknown standards. Therefore, these *individuals* are sent off based upon measurements that allow them to identify their known abilities. For example, the construction of a spaceship and its propulsion system has no validity in its quality until it is tested against some other standards of distance, time, speed, life support, and exploration qualities. They cannot find out those things unless they fire off, leave, and go out to some other place and find out what works, how well it works, and what they are going to have to do to revise it. Measurement is in absolute support of the exploration principle.

Affect* is the third reason for movement out, although probably not as strong. Often they will make trips to establish

---

* In Metaphysical writing, "affect" as a verb is carefully chosen, even where conventional grammar may indicate otherwise.

what the affects will be on them, and their affect on certain areas. This is especially true for Type A and Type B, the intra-galaxial types. They definitely use other parts of the galaxy and solar system for the sole purpose to measure affects. For example, how close can you fly to the sun without burning up? How many vortexes can you zip in and out of without having to change propulsion methods? What kind of an affect can you have on an area? What kind of an affect does the area have on you? If we landed on that little speck of an island they call Planet Earth, how long can we stay there and maintain operational efficiency?

Control is the fourth reason for movement out and is more associated with Type B, intra-galaxial negatives. The object of their mission is very definitely to take control of certain spatial areas in terms of asteroids, planets, or solar systems. I am very reluctant to use the word 'conquer'... very reluctant. It would be the wrong word because in all my experience with them I have not known them to operate in any kind of a system in which conquering is a dominant factor. I have never known *Star Wars*, but I would be foolish to say that does not occur. I have just never had any experience with them, which goes to say that they are not prevalent in and around this galaxy. Control is a factor but not a conquering factor.

My first incident was negative in terms of control, and I will let you know they had all the advantage. There was *nothing* that I could have done mentally, physically, or spiritually, (or whatever) in terms of resistance or retaliation. In a case like that, we can't talk about conquering. That is a foolish word. They had control. They didn't need to conquer me. They had enough control so that it wasn't a question if I could fight back in that regard. As I said, this is a Type B negative situation. There is an exception: If a star system (solar system) was getting into a state of such imbalance that its fragility was threatened, Type C's and Type D's would move in to take control in order to maintain galaxial harmony and alleviate the so-called ripple effect. When you throw a rock into the pond, you get ripples all the way to the edge of the pond. When a star system starts blowing up, you are going to get a galaxial effect going out interminably into space. If that were to occur, Type C and Type D spacecraft would move in to stop the ripple effect.

The best example I can give in those terms is if we brought ourselves to a high degree of nuclear capability and used that ability to such an extent that it was totally destructive to this planet. That type of event would send shock waves throughout the solar system (star system) and into the galaxy. There is better than a fifty-fifty chance that we would have Type C and Type D taking control to prevent that from occurring.

Colonization in order to establish a base is the fifth reason for movement out. Colonization is not unusual and occurs more often than you would think. We have a lot of celestial bodies out there that are not colonized, all of which have some very interesting aspects. A great many of them contain minerals way beyond our knowledge. Those components are formidable agents for some other star systems and some other galaxies.

What you want to realize is that there isn't a map coming out of a star system. When you take off you don't know where the hell you are going. You have a good idea of where you want to go, but you really don't know where you *are* going or what you are going to run into. You can get into all sorts of situations that can lead you a few hundred light years away from where you think you should have been. Unless Planet Earth became an important beacon station, there wouldn't be any sense to colonize here. Coming here would be more to study certain phenomenon that they don't have on their star base, and that does not qualify for colonization.

Remember: All celestial bodies have consciousness assigned to them; but there again, it may not be in a physical form for consciousness to use, and the form may not provide consciousness with any resistance.

Base Colonization

My experience with these *individuals* is that they do not colonize permanently. They might colonize for one or two hundred years at a time, but their whole intention when leaving home base is not to stay away indefinitely. Their purpose is generally scientific. Sometimes it is for balancing purposes and sometimes nothing more than a way station that acts as a beacon point – a lighthouse if you will – on heavily traveled space highways.

Colonization is a very difficult process because it has to include life support systems. In many cases extraterrestrials are colonizing an area alien to their home base that requires a very involved life support maintenance program. That is not easy. I remember a long conversation I had with one of the Master Commanders. He said that you have no idea about the difficulty and the amount of work that has to go into the support systems for colonization. It can take seventy to seventy-five years of earth time to just prepare for it. It is not that simple.

Consider what it would be like if we were to colonize the moon. We have to have a gravitational system. The body has to go through biological and physiological changes that might make the astronauts incompetent and unable to work. Then, we have to have a basic food system and an air system. How are you going to design a maintenance system for a one-hundred-year colonization? If you are just talking money, it would take more money than the earth has. The cost would be astronomical, although they are not necessarily looking at it in terms of cost. They are looking at it in terms of work and ability. Okay, so throw out the dollars and ask what it would take to prepare for one to two hundred years and include the enormous work force of people to maintain it.

The idea that many of Type A and Type B vehicles would be interested in colonizing a base on earth is ridiculous. First of all, earth is a very small space. We are heavily populated and we are not virgin in terms of the planet itself. We have used most of it. Also, we don't have any of the metals that they want. However, the thing that really keeps them off (and is the most damaging situation) is the high degree of variables and variations here. Their concept of having to go through seasonal changes is nothing they can cope with, as well as, the variations in the growing process we go through from childhood to old age.

On the other hand, we *are* worth studying because we are unique. The ability for us to manage these variations (including weather changes) is outrageous to them. They don't have anything near those capabilities. Another variation is that we can burn ourselves and new skin grows back. That doesn't happen on other star bases. Propagation, pregnancy, and the delivery of children fascinate them. They would very much like to know how to incorporate our variable capabilities into their system. Imagine how this would modify, if not radicalize, their ability to operate. It means they could stay out longer. They would be able to go through more vortexes and come up with greater distances with fewer problems. At this stage of the game, it would be too difficult for them to establish a base here.

Identifying Characteristics

Logically, this now brings us to some identity characteristics, which is another one of those areas where I scratch my head and ask myself, "How am I going to explain this?" First of all, the types of individuals can range from physical to non-physical. The Type A and Type B intra-galaxial individuals tend to be in the semi-physical range. Type C and Type D inter-galaxial individuals tend not to be physical, although they are what we call a compacted energy structure. This means that they can take formation of a certain type if they wish to do so. The type you see in the movies are what I would refer to as intra-galaxial types with the big heads and some semblance of a face and arms. Spacecraft *individuals* always have mass energy forms. They can even appear as light forms but not necessarily physical forms. This depends on the characteristics of their particular galaxy.

The male and female characteristics are important. It is true that wherever you go in the Universe, you are going to get a polarity situation, although you may not identify it as male or female. You are going to get plus and minus or male and female characteristics. This is true in ninety percent of all the places I have ever been. Those who do not have a physical body still have a plus and minus gene compound structure to identify them as male or female. It also happens to be true that, for the most part, male type *individuals* (as opposed to female types) conduct space travel. The reason for this is that the gene structure in energy form (in consciousness form) goes through high radiation stress during flights, regardless if that is a short or long trip.

There is a tendency for the masculine structure (whatever that might be from that galaxy) to be able to resist high radiation stress better than the female structure. I am *not* talking about radiation affecting babies or reproduction.

I *am* talking about the general stress conditions. There is a bio-nefarious radial form. These are the words they give to the action that takes place on the energy form during travel. It is the identification upon genetic mass structural change that is usually brought about as a combination of speed, distance of travel, and the propulsion systems. It just so happens that the male energy form tends to be more resistant to this than the female energy form. That does not mean to say that they don't use females, but they are used sparingly. To this day, in my contacts, I have not seen more than four females used. Again, that does not mean much because my exposure is certainly not in the upper class of everything there is to see. I do not mean to infer there is anything wrong with females. It is not at all unlikely that since the females would not be the travelers, they would be in administrative control at home base. Administrative control is an important part of the life support systems.

One of the little known stories of our astronauts going to the moon has yet to be published. There are tremendous changes that take place for them physically and in consciousness. Didn't it ever occur to you that we spend hundreds of millions of dollars to send astronauts into space, and then they retire after two or three missions? This has got to raise a lot of questions. Why does this happen? How come they don't take more missions after all that training? The reason is that the stress of space travel from here to the moon (which is like going down the front steps to extraterrestrials) is enormous. In terms of cellular molecular structure, there is no question that the human system undergoes outrageous types of stress; and we are just using a simple propulsion system. We are not using radiation systems at all.

The ability to withstand the stress becomes a major factor. Also, it tends to honestly stereotype a lot of your space *individuals.* They do tend to be categorized because it takes a certain type of *individual* to deal with the energy stress that occurs. What you are looking at is a group of highly trained celestial *individuals* that tend to fall within a general category. The types I have run into are strong, independent, opinionated, very aggressive, and non-emotional, dominant types.

Another thing you have to consider is the effect of light travel. A light year is 5.8 trillion miles. Some ships will travel that in a short period of time and others won't. What is the aging factor to the traveler who is in space for an elongated period of time? It can be enormous.

Command Structure

The command structure is different from galaxy to galaxy, but there are four major *individuals* that should be discussed. I have taken their categories and changed them semantically in order that we can talk about them. I want to see if I can give you a broader picture. Unlike *Star Trek*, there are no captains, per se, as we think about captains.

1. The Master Commander

The highest level of a star traveler is a Master Commander. This is a human term, but it fits as well as anything else I know. He is the Chief Commander who has command over everything and anything that he gets involved in, which includes his vehicle but is not exclusive to the spacecraft. In a very real sense, the Master Commanders are trained for the job from the time they are born. This is a stupid statement because they are not 'born' in the way we are. From the time of their initiation, they are claimed as Master Commanders with certain qualifications done genetically. It is not necessary for a Master Commander to have technical knowledge, but it is necessary for him to have absolute command and decision-making capabilities. Actually, I am understating the case. He is an administrator of significant worth. He has to make absolute decisions, and he cannot afford hindsight. When you are traveling twice the speed of light while moving through vortexes into galaxies, there is no time to look back and say, " I wonder if we should have…..?" That just cannot be done! Therefore, one of the Master Commander's marked qualities is that he has no sense of self-recrimination. He moves. He makes his decisions regardless, and he follows up on those decisions immediately. That takes a particular strength of character. You and I tend to look at it in the way we deal with ourselves. These are not the same types of *individuals* as we are. We have analytical views with hindsight and foresight. Basically, these *individuals* are not that type at all.

Master Commanders are the ultimate in terms of space travel and decisions. Consequently, they do get respect wherever they go because of their level of understanding. A Master Commander also holds the importance and quality of his position wherever he goes. He must be treated accordingly. For instance, this means that a Master Commander, let's say out of Star Base A, can evoke a decision on Star Base B which is not his Star Base. Unless it is ruled over by another Master Commander, it MUST be followed. I have never seen, nor can I relate to you, the kind of power Master Commanders "command". We are not even close to that kind of system. If we got beyond the moon, we would soon find out the power of a Master Commander. Boy, would we ever find out about that kind of power and in a hurry!

I couldn't think of standing face-to-face in front of a Master Commander after he made a decision and say, "Do I have to do that? Why do I have to do that?" That is inconceivable! No one would do that. The authority he transmits transcends any foolishness. In fact, the presence of these individuals is just so overwhelming that you simply don't fool around. This is the difference between where they are and where we are. Would you ask an Avatar why He is doing what He is doing?

Master Commanders do have ratings and those ratings are known by a certain auric level of energy. They are super level type *individuals* who never misuse their power. As a matter of fact, Type C and Type D Master Commanders can invoke their position against Type A and Type B <u>intra</u>-galaxial Commanders because one Master Commander recognizes the level of the next one. No one <u>ever</u> questions the order of a Master Commander. My impression with a Master Commander is that he is an absolute power and force. I have never known a Master Commander to be married. <u>Never</u>. An average star base might have about thirty Master Commanders, and that is assuming the star base is sending out a lot of vehicles.

2. The Agent

In the structure of the system, you will find what I am going to call an Agent. The Agent has a second in command administrative post. He is normally the prime representative from the star base. He is not a political type. He *is* the *individual* who represents the star base law as it pertains to the galaxial mission. He is probably more educated and more infused with the content of the mission than the Master Commander himself in relationship to the intent of the star base.

Here is where we have to get over a minor problem. We tend to think these *individuals* just take off for the hell of it. This is not true. Every ship that leaves their star base is on a mission. They know what they are going for, and they know the trajectories. They know the prime requirements and what they want to bring back. The Agent is responsible for the maintenance of that mission's intent. He is the advisor to the Master Commander. I am sure I have made this clear by now, but the Agent cannot override the Master Commander.

3. The Master Technical Officer

The other person worth bringing up is the Master Technical Officer. He is from the star base and is completely trained in the construction of the ship, its gear, and its equipment. This is why the Master Commander doesn't have to fool with it, or he would go crazy. The Master Commander has to concentrate on what is going on with all things being considered, somewhat like a computer. He has to come up with immediate answers. Therefore, he has got to have the Master Technical Officer on board ship with the job to know how the ship runs and to keep it running. Obviously, the Master Technical Officer has a lot of *individuals* helping him, but he is one of the prime officers.

4. The Arbitrator

The fourth prime officer is the Arbitrator. This is an individual who is trained in inter-galaxial law. That statement is ridiculous because basically there isn't any inter-galaxial law. However, the Arbitrator's job is to interpret the conditions and the laws that exist as the ship moves from galaxy to galaxy and from point to point.

Suppose you have a Type C ship arrive here on Planet Earth. It isn't the Master Commander's job to determine what is right and what is wrong as it pertains to how he conducts the mission at this point. That determination is the job of the Arbitrator. It is up to the Arbitrator to be knowledgeable about what the galaxial law is in this galaxy and, therefore, what the planetary laws are on earth as a Star Base. The Arbitrator passes that information along to the Master Commander. He says, in effect, "Here are certain things you should not do, or certain things you can do." The Master Commander makes his decision according to that information.

Just as all the other officers, the Arbitrator is trained from birth for his job. His whole life is spent in what I will call 'inter-galaxial law travel'. That is a terrible term, but I couldn't come up with anything else. The Arbitrator carries an enormous amount of weight. In many cases, I've seen the Master Commanders who would not circumvent the advice of the Arbitrator. However, it is never the decision on the part of the Arbitrator. The advice he offers to the Master Commander is usually the basis for the final decision because he studies inter-galaxial systems regarding what can and cannot be expected.

In every major ship, you will find these four officers. Frankly, the major spaceships are Type C and Type D inter-galaxial ships. You will not find them on Type A or Type B intra-galaxial spaceships. Think about this as the difference between pilots who fly Air West from Los Angeles to Las Vegas and those captains who fly Pan American from San Francisco to Australia. You just don't see a pilot flying a two-engine plane five thousand miles. I have never seen these positions filled by a female. I have a pretty strong indication that I never will see them flown by a female because of the high-energy stress on the construction of the *individuals.* It is for that reason that females are not born or trained to take on these assignments.

I would like to point out that the *individuals* never leave once they are in these positions. They will spend their whole lifetime (whatever that might be) in that position. We might be talking five or six hundred earth years or more. By the way, you should know that earth is designed for a three-hundred-year life span. We are obviously not anywhere near that point. If we were where we should be and at our ultimate, we would be running three hundred years for each lifetime. If we had a Master Commander out of here, he would be in the job for three hundred years, more or less.

I have found all four of these officers to be very self-sufficient. If you were to ask me the most outstanding characteristics of these types (outside of their great sense of self-sufficiency), I would say it is their sense of manners and style that comes through almost immediately. They know how to handle outrageous power with a delicacy that surpasses anything I have ever seen. I have never seen the power used irrationally or in excess, yet I have always seen it used. It is there.

Time Warp

First of all, we have to change the way we think about time as we view it. We deal on the basis of years tied to the earth's trip around the sun every 365 days. That is a construct of a year. Obviously, it becomes evident that an inter-galaxial vehicle couldn't possibly use that kind of timing. Their star system is probably not revolving around anything close to this. If it is, it may be something closer to a few thousand years in one revolution.

Space vehicles operate in warp time. Warp time is based on a vortex. It is the time necessary to clear a single vortex. The way this works is that the vortex is a compact of energy that

Extraterrestrial Activities 33

has a magnetic center. Regardless of the size of the vortex, the time it takes for a space vehicle to move through the vortex is the time scale. The Universal system of cycles is all dependent upon vortexes, therefore the time scale does not change as we would imagine that it would change due to small and large vortexes.

What constitutes a Universal cycle? A Universal cycle constitutes the distance between the positive and negative polarity. <u>Remember</u>: Vortexes can have many different shapes. They can look like very odd things and do very odd things, but they *always* have a positive and a negative polarity. The time element of the spaceship is registered in vortexual movement. The reason for this is that X amount of propulsion energy produces X amount of bio-stress on the occupants. Therefore, a Master Commander would say something like, "We have been out 257 voti." Those are my words not his. He is conveying that he, his occupants, and his ship have gone through 257 transfer cycles.

If you knew anything about galaxial travel, you would say, "WOW!" Even a single vortex transfer is going to be terrific. We have nothing to compare with this so let me give you some examples. Let's say that you are in the presence of a very overpowering human being. They take everything away from you and superimpose their desires upon you. Is it not true that just five minutes around a person like that can exhaust you? What is happening is that you are feeling the vortex of that person. You are, in effect, transferring through that vortex. If you have some idea of how exhausting this is, you can get an idea of what the stress is of a spacecraft going through a vortex. They also must be able to deal with the vortexual stress of what they are passing through. In order to space travel you must pass through vortexes. If you are talking about skirting a vortex in space travel, it cannot be done. That would be impossible. Each vortex constitutes a time element. Sometimes spaceships will be prepared to make a trip fitted out for a fifteen-vortex trip. That is it. After that, the spacecraft has to go back to their star base because there isn't any support system beyond a fifteen-vortex trip.

Distance effects are secondary. The propulsion system will not carry the spaceship through every element of the galaxy through which it travels. It runs into atmospheric changes, and there are parts of galaxies where there is a fluid heavier than water in the air space. Spacecraft would have to fly through those conditions. The point regarding distance is that there are particular elements that prevent a ship from going out a certain distance because they don't have the propulsion system to come back. Supposedly, this is in the design of the mission before they go, but (for the most part) they don't really know what they are going to run into. They may have a lot of information, but they *really* don't know because the vortex does not remain stable. Atmospheres do not remain stable.

Now we can go back to the old question of why we don't see a couple hundred spaceships a month. Getting in here and getting out is the problem. On Earth we have a very heavy electrically charged atmosphere. Let me tell you, that can give them a lot of headaches. It can use up a huge amount of propulsion system capabilities at a rate four times the normal usage, although this is not fuel per se. I am referring to Planet Earth and its atmosphere, but we have to look at this in context to their Star Base, their star system, their conditions, and their atmosphere. They have to be highly prepared, and they are not always prepared to do what is required. This is one more reason why we don't have them scooting around the skies playing games. It isn't that easy!

If I were a Master Commander and I knew I wanted to make a trip to this galaxy and I was shooting for this star system,

I would say the flat base preparations would include thousands of safe guards, not to mention, the enormous amount of time for the preparations. Even then, I wouldn't get on board thinking that I had it made. I am saying this from what I know from living here and being here. Coming into this kind of a star system, I would be very concerned about my propulsion stress because of the heavily charged electrical atmosphere.

Sunspots

The sunspots also play havoc with the requirements of the propulsion system. It would be highly questionable if *anybody* would want to get mixed up in those sunspots in terms of coming into such a star system. Sunspots throw out electrically charged particles into the ionic atmosphere that have a strong affect on our weather and on our electrical communication systems. This has a very strong ecological effect in terms of ionization and de-ionization characteristics. Sunspots are always a problem. When they get very big, they can be extremely serious in terms of atmospheric balance. We still don't know how strong those effects are going to be, and I don't know of any Type C spaceships that have crashed here. I am not saying there haven't been any, I just don't know of any. Type A and Type B intra-galaxial crafts have crashed here.

The time and distance effects on all the craft occupancy related to vortexual motion might have the senior officers in fairly good shape after a trip of fourteen-vortexes, but you could have a breakdown on the crew. They can't do anything they want (as we think they can) since there are a great number of problems to deal with.

Transmitting Stations

1. Transmitters

Star Base Type C has acquired a very interesting and somewhat phenomenal, if not radical, system. High-speed star based *individuals* have been able to establish the authority to incarnate individuals. There are people walking planet earth who are just like you and me. They are alive. They come into a normal birth incarnating the same way we do. They bleed like we do, they are human, and they have had previous lives. They are here now. For whatever reasons before they came, they were hooked into a Type C star base project. In so doing, they accept a certain frequency rate that is a bit different than yours and mine. They are active transmitters of information, and they provide signals to Type C *individuals* and ships without necessarily knowing it.

I must say, they tend to be rather odd-type people. They are on a mission, which means that they do not have learning lessons, per se, like the rest of us. Rather than having a karmic life lesson to learn, they agree (and the etheric energies agree) that this will be their mission as part of their whole training. They are transmitting stations for frequency rates that measure frequency conditions for the part of the planet they are on and their surrounding area. One of them can transmit from quite a wide range such as the southwest area of the United States, but you must consider that is not a very large area in relation to the whole world.

They certainly know that they are a bit odd, but they accept that as if they are alright and everybody else is the odd one. One of their idiosyncrasies (if not their problem) is that they tend to walk around a bit blown out most of the time because they operate at a frequency rate some thirty to forty percent higher than most of us. I have identified one in the work I have done who is pretty sane compared to most others. He is pretty stable – not too stable, but pretty stable. Some of the others are really on a high wire. They are beeping and bleeping all the time. You can hardly miss all sorts of signals they are sending out. However, nobody pays much attention to them. They have been borrowed from other galaxies, which is part of their experiential knowledge. This had to be okayed from the etheric level (and it is okayed) because Type C and Type D star basers must send out informational contact in galaxies of importance. We are just one little spot in this whole thing. There are hundreds of thousands of these individuals spread out across the galaxy. We don't have many on earth, but we do have some. They are, in effect, sending stations. They do transmit vital frequency information from this planet to star bases Type C and Type D, which is primarily used to maintain a balance portion of the galaxy.

It is the responsibility of the *individuals* running the galaxy to maintain balance. Therefore, they have a system and these mission-type individuals are part of that system. Nevertheless, they are as human as you and me. They have jobs. They eat and sleep, and they have some fun while operating on very high frequencies.

2. Cloning

The star based, high-speed *individuals* also have a cloning capability. We have more clones here out of Type A and Type B than we have transmitters who are here from Type C and Type D and on mission-type lives. I do not know how many, but I do know there are a good number of cloned individuals who are operating on earth who are not human. They were not born. They are cloned from Type A and Type B star bases. They too are acting like transmitters.

You see, Type A and Type B cannot have transmitters of the kind that I have just described. Therefore, in order to set up their own kind of transmitting stations, they do it by the cloning affect. These individuals do not come in as little children and grow up. They appear at any age they want to; they can be male or female. If you at all sensitive to them, they can be identified. They have an unusual quality about them, but it is not an etheric quality. It is a non-human quality. They tend to look too perfect in many ways, and they most always give you some indication of non-emotionalism. A better way of putting this is to say that if you watch them, you will see that their reaction to people around them is not the same as ours.

A situation stands out very vividly in my mind. I was at the air terminal in New York, and I was waiting for a change of planes. I had about an hour so I wandered down to the main terminal to people watch. While I was watching people, one of them showed up. You couldn't miss him. If you looked at everyone around him, you could see he wasn't reacting the way everyone else was reacting. Neither was he acting as someone who might have control over his emotions. It was totally obvious that he was just non-human. His movements, his facial expressions, and his reactions to what was going on with the people next to him were different without being mechanical.

Clones are more easily spotted in a group. They talk as you and I talk, but their speech is more modulated with less inflection due to the lack of emotionalism. Type D star based individuals usually pick super attractive people to use as a pattern for cloning. They match the cell structure of a person. If they wanted to clone off you, they would do it while you are sleeping. It doesn't hurt you. They are just using you as a pattern. The simplest method is a scan beam that registers all the values of the cell, and they literally build a pattern from that. Then the pattern is set up on an electrical grid. The grid is placed over one of their *individuals,* and they go through a transforming process that is not very difficult at all. The person literally picks up all of your patterns. They have your characteristics, and they will look almost like an identical twin. To my knowledge, they never use the clone in the same area where they were cloned. What they are looking for is frequency rate types more than anything else. They are looking for types whose general structure and physical wherewithal is such that it produces a certain frequency rate. There is no way to stop the cloning, nor is there any need to do so. Cloning is not a hard operation when you understand the technicalities.

3. Specific Mission Life : In cooperation with the etheric Hierarchy and star base Type C and Type D

I cannot pass this point along without also bringing up one more aspect that is very, very important. There are a number of incidents that occur during periods of time in which Star Base C and Star Base D will work in cooperation with the etheric Hierarchy to support, change, or upset the life of a human being who is here on a specific mission-type life. I do not know how many. Let me put it this way: Let's say Rick has not been born yet, and he is still in the etheric state. He goes to look at his overall pattern before he incarnates and is told that in the early part of his life (the first thirty years) he will go through a normal human process. After his thirtieth birthday, he is to start on a mission and this mission is basically an etheric mission that he is agreeing to do. They also tell him that in order for him to make that transition, it is necessary to bring in some other effects during the thirtieth year to get him to transmit from who he was to who he is going to be. That will include Star Base Type C or Type D elements to aid in that transmission. Type C or Type D can aid in that transmission by some cloning work that may be far out in years, or they can just upset the conditions in his life in such a way that he makes major transitional changes. He will have no idea how it could have happened that way. The star base *individuals* make those changes happen in support of the mission. They literally get involved. Needless to say, this does not occur frequently. This is not a common occurrence, but it does happen, and it happens enough times within a decade to make it worthy of note in covering this material. It will happen with certain people on mystical missions, or etheric missions, or metaphysical missions. It could happen sometimes with certain science types. Obviously, it is reserved for those missions that require monumental changes either in personality and/or life conditions.

What you need to understand is that once any one is released from the etheric area, the etheric entities can only advise. They cannot affect and interfere to override your will. As a matter of fact, the etheric 'people' cannot do a heck of a lot of manipulating, except in patterns of energy. If human manipulation has to be applied in a positive way <u>for the mission</u>, that has got to come out of Star Base C or D. This is a mission-type thing only. The mission is the reason they are included. There isn't anyone on the planet that can take over that job. This would never be entrusted even to Type A or Type B <u>intra</u>-galaxial *individuals* because they don't have the wherewithal. It has to come out of an <u>inter</u>-galaxial quality. That is in the Plan, and it is not anything that is just sprung upon a person clear out of the blue. It is written up and approved upon etherically before the mission person physically incarnates.

I have only seen this happen a couple of times, and I have talked to Master Commanders about this point. I have also talked to the entities 'Upstairs' about this. It has to be set up ahead of time and followed through with when the time comes. It is dated for a specific time in a person's life, regardless of what is going on. It will occur at that time, no matter what, because the Star Base Type C or Type D are committed to that timing cycle. The mission individual may not be ready for the transition. My experience is that they are most often not ready for it. Nevertheless, it occurs and blows their whole life apart. It can be anything. It could be a change of people in their lives, a change of locale, a change of work, or it could be a cloning operation of some sort. It could be a manifestation or a visitation. You *must* realize that not every mission is going to be involved in this type activity.

Let me reiterate. This is only used when it becomes necessary for the materiality of the mission to be established in definitive form. That means the changing of physicality relative to the individual's life requires major changes that must be made in order for the mission to go on. These changes cannot be done by the etheric level because the etheric level cannot ever interfere. The etheric area can set up energy patterns to support it, but they cannot force the changes. Star Base C or D actually forces the changes. This can run the range from the human being seriously ill and almost dying to wiping out a whole family. The list is without limits. Whatever is necessary to bring these phenomenal changes about occurs and the person's life takes a completely different path.

There is a definite difference between the type of mission life that has Star Base Type C and Type D support in cooperation with the etheric support and the mission life that does not run into any star base support. Those without the star base support come into the mission at an early age and generally ease themselves into the mission. You can watch these children easily developing into their mission around age thirteen, fourteen, or fifteen. Their leadership begins to show. The mission-types described in this section are the types that either look pretty normal (or abnormal in a negative sort of way). Then, all of a sudden at X years they hit an absolute breaking point. Their life totally changes to be completely different.

What I have given you are the three elements that have a very active affect on this planet. The one element is where transmitters are used. The other is where cloning is used, and the third is where there is support of a mission-type life in cooperation with Star Base C and Star Base D and in cooperation with the etheric Hierarchy.

Negative Effects

One of the problems of Star Base Type B <u>intra</u>-galaxial negatives is that they tend to use their influence against scientific development. Either they want to accelerate the effect for their own reasons, or they tend to want to retard it for their own reasons. Many times failures in our space program that cannot be explained by any other method could well have been affected by Type B negatives interference. This could be a rocket that doesn't make it into orbit, spaceships that don't function properly, scientists who say there is no cure for cancer, and diets that say it is okay to live on a diet of hot dogs and you will live forever. These are often the kinds of influence from Type B <u>intra</u>-galaxial negative.

Mind you, in no way am I saying that negative influence is being used everyday. I am indicating that Type B <u>does try</u> to exercise (and not always successfully) that type of influence. When they do, it is usually through the scientific community. They do this in order to get a developmental system here that suits their control means, whatever those means may be. They are trying to maintain some kind of control effort over where we are going scientifically. Also, they may want to support their own research, perhaps in terms of finding out how we function in our experience.

I have seen Type B <u>intra</u>-galaxial negatives use control against other elements, but on the scale of one hundred percent, they will use control efforts about ninety-two percent of the time within the scientific area. I think most of their effort is in holding us back in the <u>intra</u>-galaxial travel. For example, we were pouring billions of dollars into the space program, and almost out of the clear blue sky the program was cut. We were told by the new administration in Washington D. C. that there was no more money to do that type of thing. The space program was temporarily discontinued. Any thinking person realizes that one of the most magnificent efforts of modern times is made going from here to the moon (and all that goes along with that in creating new products to improve our daily experience). I will tell you that I am sure this was an example of Type B interference. There was energy exercised effectively enough to cause people in responsible positions to change direction.

This occurs in the same way that it may not be your plans to be affected by me, but you will be if you don't do anything to exercise your will and stop my affect upon you. You become receptive to me and you will be affected. That would be evident in your inability to maintain your plan. My plan to affect you was working. If your plan is not working, that is up to you. When you have receptivity, you are involved to one degree or another and in one way or another.

In the long run, I am not concerned about Type B effects. We are getting (and will continue to get) a lot of Type C and Type D support. This means that whatever influence Type A and Type B exert will be nominal by comparison because Type C and Type D are superior in knowledge and ability.

Ship Construction

The outer element of the ships is made out of skin using a thermonuclear base. Next to the outer wall is the inner wall made of palladium. This buffer wall has the properties of both water and lead for the purpose of keeping the thermonuclear area from the inner liner. The inner liner is a mixture of a plastic-mineral combination. All the conditions on the ship are impervious to nuclear energy.

The construction of the large Mother Ships can take as long as 17,000 earth years of time. Obviously, you can realize why they don't fire off many of them, and why we don't see many of them around. There are a few of them being built, but the amount of work is enormous for such enormous size ships. The size of the individuals on board varies according to the galaxies they come from. I consider them, on the average, to be about six feet tall since my experience with them has been in the six-foot category. That might be because that is my size category. There are some experiences I have had with ships where the individuals are eight or nine feet tall.

Propulsion Systems

The size of the spaceship is relative to the propulsion system. That is based on the over-all intention of their mission. How much vortexual energy they have to deal with determines how long they intend to be gone. The propulsion for most ships is from a central radial-reactive, self-compensatory, auto-gravitational, anti-magnetic system. I am trying to get this down into usable terms, and it isn't that hard to understand. The word radial is the worst word in that explanation because it pertains a lot to what you know, and extraterrestrials are a bit beyond what you know. However, it does indicate a radial frequency range. In other words, the propulsion system is a self-compensatory frequency operated reactor. Self-compensating is like a breather reactor. It produces as much energy as it uses up. It never loses energy. For every ounce of energy it uses, it produces an ounce of energy. That is self-compensatory energy. Auto-gravitational means it has the ability to use the gravitational flow of energy forms within its vortex. Anti-magnetic flow means it cannot de-magnetize which would be the worse thing you could have on a ship; that would destroy its propulsion system.

Another reason you don't see many spaceships around here is that earth is a highly magnetic planet. This is NOT the best place for these ships because magnetism does affect their reactive systems that are based on anti-magnetic propulsion systems. The ships cannot be magnetized and still function. I have seen more than a dozen propulsion centers, and I have never seen two exactly alike. They all seem to have something of a basic core center. The only thing I can think of that is similar is a nuclear reactor.

The propulsion systems are all contained in a special metal and are almost always in the center of the ship. I can only think of two cases where I saw it off center, and they were smaller ships. The energy is passed from the propulsion system to the rest of the ship by flow openings through which the energy moves down through these openings. In other words, it comes off the center reactor as an opening, but not as a built-in tube because it is molded into the ship itself. The energy flows along this pathway to wherever it is going to be used.

The activity, in terms of propulsion to star systems, is primarily an up and down system (not forward, backwards, or side-ways). It tends to move the ship helicopter style. It is not so much that the ship spins, but the propulsion systems are set into a spinning motion. They tend to produce a spinning top affect, which is the only thing they can use to travel through vortexes. Since all vortexes are spinning, you could not put a ship into one vortex on a linear basis, or it would tumble the ship over and over and over. Therefore, the ship must be prepared in its propulsion system to match the vortex. The only thing that will match the vortex is a ship that is also spinning at the same rate as the vortex. Therefore, we have a situation where we have a vortex that is spinning and the ship is spinning at the same rate. When the ship enters the vortex, it is either spinning at the same motion as the vortex or, in some cases, it will spin counter to the vortex motion. It must spin.

The spinning effect is not the spin of the ship. The spin of the propulsion system has an opening to the top and the bottom of the ship. If we were looking at it, we would swear that the ship is spinning; however, the center propulsion center is spinning. If you want to look at it in those terms, it means the outer ship then remains fairly stable. This is why reports sighting ships indicate that the ship went straight up, or that the ship moved at a rapid rate forward, but upwards. You see, the greatest speed of the ship is up and down because of the way the propulsion system is set up. It does move forward in the same aerodynamic way as a helicopter moves forward, but its great speed is vertical speed due to the design of the propulsion system.

In some cases, the ship emits a lot of light and color. Some of it is almost noiseless, although, I suppose there is a sense of humming. Now we lack words. If you were in space where there is an average amount of noise, and then you went into a totally silent room, you would actually sense that you hear sounds. You don't really hear them. There is a kind of funny echo sound that is in your head. As a matter of fact, when you stay in a totally silent room, you hear the humming as a background sound. This is what most of the propulsion systems on the spacecraft sound like. When you first get onto the ship, the sense is you've just walked into a totally quiet room. There is an echo sound. You feel it almost as much as you hear it. The propulsion system is built to last the lifetime of the ship. Generally, it does not need any repair work. The only time that it would need extra work is if their magnetic system was broken down, or they entered a vortex they couldn't deal with.

In my experience, I have never seen a ship that was ever armed. I have never seen anything that indicates push/pull buttons or laser (or whatever that might be) because the spaceships never go out on that kind of a mission. I have never seen a *Star Wars*-type situation. In that respect, I don't think they are capable of handling something like that. I have never discussed this with a Master Commander because I think it would be bad manners to do so.

The average propulsion system on a large Mother Ship is designed to last about 20,000 years without overhaul, refueling, or repair. Again, that figure is based on the average amount of space travel without any unusual circumstances. Terminology is bad because they don't operate on the basis of years. They decide what size ship they want according to what it is meant to do. They decide what kind of propulsion they need in order to do that mission based on the number of vortexes they have to transfer through. It is all put together figuring that is the life of the ship. They may be talking five thousand, twenty thousand, or fifteen thousand years.

Their purpose isn't the way we would see it. We might look off to Mars and say, "We want to explore Mars." Their target area is a much larger scope. They are talking about galaxial travel, where we are only talking about solar system travel. Hell, they take a whole star base to build their ships!

Ship Size

The size of the ship is based upon the amount of independent time that it is designed to operate. Independent time means the amount of time away from its star base. Here I have to use a new word. The word that they use translates to a word called 'grelude'. One grelude equals 170 light years. One light year is 5.8 trillion miles. One grelude is 170 x 5.8 trillion. That is the mile distance used. Type A and Type B <u>intra</u>-galaxial ships have the maximum size of 10 greludes. Type C ships are sized at 902 greludes, and Type D ships,which are the cosmic ships, are sized at 14,000 greludes. What you are looking at is the ship size with the independent time it can operate.

Let's take Type D, cosmic ships. You have to multiply 14,000 times 170 light years. Since one light year is 5.8 trillion miles, you have to multiply that times the result you get from the first multiplication. That is the distance the ship is built to operate. Now you can understand why it takes thousands of years to build a ship. Type D ships are going to be built to operate into the depths of the Universe and back again. They can be thousands of miles long if they are built to operate at maximum, but they don't have to be that large. There tends to be a limit, so they say, on what they want to build. Again, that is based on the mission. They are operating in an infinite Universe, so size in an infinite Universe doesn't mean anything. The mission is based on how far they want to travel.

You have 14,000 x 170 light years. Therefore, what you have is two million, three hundred thousand light years times 5.8. Type D ships are the maximum built and can travel thirteen million, eight hundred and four thousand trillion miles. If you round that off, it is 13.8 million, trillion miles. If you take a Type A ship, which in <u>intra</u>-galaxial, we are talking

1700 times 5.8, so we are talking 9860 trillion miles for it to operate at a maximum, independent travel distance. Considering the star base, you use up an astronomical amount of miles. This is like running around the corner to the grocery store using miles like raindrops.

To do basic exploration in this star base alone, you are going to start using hundreds of millions of miles before you even turn around. Think about what it would be to explore a couple of galaxies! You could use up nine hundred trillion miles in no time at all. This gives us a perspective that using this amount of mileage isn't really as wild as you might think.

Ship's Compliment

The average ship complement for a Type A ship of 10 greludes is 827 inhabitants (travelers, crew, and what have you). For Type C ships, the average crew is 1011 inhabitants. For Type D ships, crews run from 2700 to 3200 inhabitants. All of this depends on the purpose of the mission. Nobody on the crew is a midshipman, all are highly trained. They never send out a ship as a training ship. They couldn't take the chance of having someone not knowing their job. They do all their training back in and around their star base. When they send a person out, he is qualified by whatever virtue they established as qualifications.

Probably because of my military background, the thing that impressed me on my first contact was walking in and seeing everyone so bloody efficient. Everyone knew exactly what they were doing. The whole impression was that nothing was being wasted. No one was climbing over anyone else for position. No one was expecting anyone else to do their job. Everything was *very* smooth. Everyone was in control of their own responsibility. I was overwhelmed the first time I saw that. In fact, I still am! I realized they must have gone through a really outrageous system by which they trained these individuals. Each individual does his job well without going through the emotional things we go through. Therefore, everything works harmoniously. You get the whole sense that everything is clicking.

When a Master Commander on a Mother Ship issues an order or a command, everyone knows exactly what their particular job is without any question about the command. Nobody looks over at someone else and says," Hey, what are you doing? You are pushing my buttons." Everyone knows exactly what *they* are supposed to do, and they do it instantaneously based on whatever it is they are supposed to do. It is like one fine clock going click-click-click. That is terribly impressive to me. We don't have anything that even smacks of it.

None of this is based on any kind of law or punishment system. It is training and dedication. It is an honor to be on these ships. It is a dedication that we would look at as no less than a dedication to a great spiritual adventure of our own. This is especially true out of Type D ships because they are so closely allied to Universal function. They are so large, and they have so much to do. It is all dedication with that sense of identity and that sense of fulfillment that all comes into play. This is consciousness operating at the highest peak of its creative efficiency. You just *know* it is there because it is something you feel more than you see it. Everyone knows what to do with the exception of Type B ships. I don't know about them. I am not positive about this, but I think some of the stories that came out of people who said they have been taken aboard all seem to mention that everything seems to be operating very efficiently.

Transfer of Information

All information on the flight is immediately transferred to their star base. It is done automatically on the same frequency level as the propulsion system indicates. Consequently from the initial blast off, <u>everything</u> that transpires with that ship from second to second is already recorded and known at star base. This is true whether it is good, bad, or indifferent. If you want to identify someone who is responsible for this, it would be the Agent. He is the representative of the star base, and he is responsible for the intent of the mission based on the star base intent. Therefore, he is also responsible for the record keeping of which he really doesn't have to do much because everything is automatically recorded at their star base.

My reluctance in talking to you about this is the confusion of trying to give you a picture without getting you too set in your mind because every galaxy and every star base will have variations. If you ever come across a spacecraft, you might say, "Wait until I get my hands on Gregge. He didn't say anything about this." Well, I couldn't possibly have told you because I don't know what all the variations could be. They are based on the star base of that particular galaxy. I am trying to give you a common means based on my experience and my discussions with a couple of Master Commanders who provided me with the information. I am just saying that all the discussions I have had come out to look like this. I don't know what the variances will be. I think I have already made the point that none of the senior commanders I have come across on the ships have been married in the sense of marriage. That is one of the requirements. They are not trained for marriage. What more can I say?

Navigational Systems

After you fire off, one of the most difficult things is how to navigate to get to where you are going. There are really not any good star maps. You certainly don't know what you are getting into out there. There has to be a certain amount of unknown risk error that is involved. Consequently, none of the ships navigate by any star system. How could you? Could you conceive of yourself in a large ship in the deep reaches of space with galaxies to the right of you and galaxies to the left of you and with half of these things never having been mapped out by anyone? Even if they were, how do you know orbits and vortexes haven't changed over the thousands of years? What are you going to navigate by? You *really* don't know.

The only way you can navigate is by vortexes themselves. Are you ready for that? It is really very complicated. Mother Ships have what they call hydro-ether-quantitative calculators. The reason for this is that all vortex centers contain a center magnetic line made up of a compound very similar to water and ether. Through every center of a vortex is a hydro-ether line. Those are bad words because that is not a true compound. However, that is as close as we could come. If you take the make-up of a hydrogen-nitrogen compound and the make-up of ether and combine that into a new molecular form, you would have something similar.

What a ship does for navigation is something very fascinating and intricate. You have a series of vortexes each with this hydrogen-ether line. A ship navigates down those vortexual lines. They actually navigate through the vortexual lines from one vortexual line to another vortexual line and then another and another. The line that goes through the vortex is actually magnetic in the sense that it is used as a guidance system. What you get is a series of transit plots that can be punched out on the onboard computer. By doing this, the crew can get their intersections and basically know where they have come from and where they are going.

What they are looking at on the punch-outs is a mass of dot-to-dot lines. Assuming that the start is the star base (which is logical), they can always tell where they are by tracing along the vortexual line. All that information is their log and is passed back to the main computer at star base. The log can be used by another ship if another ship wanted to follow the same vortexual lines. In this case, we are using vortexual lines in the same respect that we use galaxies as a vortex. They are passing from galaxy to galaxy using the vortex and coming right down the line. In one respect, the vortexual line of this galaxy may not even run anywhere close to where earth is located. The centerline of this galaxy may be a few million light years out, in which case the ships that are navigating are not even coming close to us. They are zipping way beyond where we would ever be. This is the only navigational system going.

I think I had better digress at this point. You have to understand that the spaceships have a computer system that is rapidly advanced from anything we know in what it can do in its dimensional speed. We tend to look at a two dimensional plane and think we have really done something if we get a three dimensional system. They have eight and nine dimensional systems, which they can superimpose one superimpositions upon another superimposition and get a total readout both visually and in actual readout form. I have no way of matching our computer systems with anything they do. We are absolutely babies. They would look at something like our calculator, and where we would say, "Isn't this marvelous?" They would see it as a hammer, chisel, and a big rock knocking out a, b, c, and d. There is simply no way to make the comparisons.

Safety Precaution

All ships, (I'm talking Types A, Types B, Types C, and Types D) have a programmed time return that cannot be overridden on board. This is their built-in safety precaution. When a ship is launched, it has built into its computer mechanism and into its propulsion system a programmed time limit return. In the event that the crew is incapacitated for some reason (or that the ship is commandeered for some reason and cannot be operated on board) the system will automatically return to base at the end of its time line limit. This is done through its automatic system unless the system has been destroyed. The chance of the system being destroyed, other than a crash, is astronomically slim.

Let me put it this way. If there is anything secret about the ship, this is the top-secret element. They build the system into the ship and there is no way to tamper with it. There is no way you can change the interlock system. There is no system by which the Master Commander has the key or that anybody else would have the key either. There is none of that. It is built right into the ship. It is programmed into the actual construction of the ship. Every time that ship takes off, the system is activated. There is no way to override that activation either at star base or on board the ship. If the ship did not return at the end of the activated time, the automatic system takes over regardless of what is going on. I have never seen one of these automatic programmed time limit systems because there is no way you can see it. This has all been told to me by the Master Commanders.

The spaceship will return to its star base on the same navigational lines on its inward leg as it was on during the out leg portion of the trip. The programmed time limit system is primarily put there in case of a true disaster. It took 17,000 years to build the ship, and they don't intend

Extraterrestrial Activities 55

to have it circle out in space forever! If, for example, a ship was commandeered and the time line ran out, there isn't anything those who commandeered it could do to override the automatic system that clicks in at the exact time. If those who commandeered it cannot live on the star base when the ship returns, they will die. Regardless, the ship will return to its home base.

There is something I need to emphasize here. The vortexes have different sizes. Sometimes both ends are about equal. Sometimes they have a big bulb in the middle. There are all sorts of shapes, but this isn't what matters. What matters is that the ship will follow the magnetic line of each vortex back to its star base. The propulsion takes over and matches the automatic system. If that means a counter-clockwise revolution, it goes counter-clockwise.

Consider that the extraterrestrials don't know what they are going to find out in space or what their vortexes are going to be. However, when they get on board they do know there is a propulsion system that cannot be tampered with or overridden. Obviously, this can add a great sense of what we would call security. The ship *will* get back because star base always knows where the ship is, and there is no possibility of it getting lost out in space because the automatic recall is built into the ship.

The time of recall is directly associated with the mission, and that is established by the star base. The Master Commander has nothing to do with the time recall. It's the star base that runs the mission out on vortexual time. If something were to happen to the crew before the time line runs out and there is no one to navigate the ship back to star base, it will then return to base at the time programmed for recall. The ship will stay in orbit until the time line runs out.

Life Support Systems

For Type A, C, and D ships there are three support systems. Obviously, life support systems depend on the needs of the *bodies* and that depends on the galaxies they come from. The Type A ships use a chemical C support system that uses mercury-type regenerators to support the life elements. This is based on a kind of electronic conductivity. Where mercury tends to poison us, mercury-type elements support life on these ships. The components of mercury are changed, but it is still mercury, and it is <u>highly</u> conductive.

Type C ships use what they call an adaptive-one system that is a laser or light based support. When I talk about life support, I mean light is their basic food support. It is a laser support system. This accounts for a lot of the stories that you hear from people who have entered or seen these ships, and they tell about this great light illumination.

Type D ships use what they call an ES-4 system, which they describe as molo-bilineal-auto-segment-atomic-refractured. The way I understand it is that this is a system by which they re-molecularize molecules into life energy. They will take a molecule of energy that is unusable in its original form and break it apart and re-molecularize it. They draw from it only the nutrients they need and leave the part they don't need to form a new molecule. It does not remain as waste. It remains as molecular energy. I am not sure what molo-bilineal means except that it is the type of system they use. The auto-segment means it is an automatic segmentation. They start the system going and then there is an automatic molecular segmentation that takes place. The atomic re-fracturing is breaking apart the molecules, taking out of it what they want and allowing the rest of it to reform itself. A terrific system! It can go for a long, long time without having to worry about it.

Communication with Planet Earth

There are five basic and common forms that they use for communication. As you well might imagine, leading the list is telepathic communication. This is simply thought transference. My very first contact of a positive nature was strictly this method, although they combined it with a laser, light beam effect. The laser beam was in line with the communication much like a cell phone. The thought transference ran down the laser and went back and forth on the laser beam itself. They imaged to me what we are as humans except more of an auric light effect. You really don't look at a body form at all. You become so involved in the harmony of contact that you stop thinking about what you look like, and you stop thinking about what they look like. Most people who have indicated that they have had saucer contact will tell you that communication was primarily telepathic. This holds true most anyplace in the Universe.

The second system they use for communication is cellular-electro-wave attachment. This is very dangerous. They actually hook you into a machine. This is the type I found Type B uses. They get you on board, they stick you in a chair, and they put electrodes on you. They actually use the impulses of mind and body. This is the same experience I had. What is wrong is that it tends to charge the system and upset the nervous system balance while they are doing it.

The cellular-electro-wave attachment system is also the method Type A and Type C would use if you were incapacitated and could not communicate with them. Then, they would hook you up, but you would not necessarily get hurt by it because there would be a read-out of what was going on in the system and on your mind. It would be used to control the energy, not to control you.

The third system they use for communication is an octave-harmonic transference. It is basically a voice system transferred to any kind of harmonic communication. We are now talking about any kind of sound such as voices and musical notes. That system can also be used, but I don't think they are capable of using it in this galaxy.

The fourth system they use for communication is a bio-chemical-partition. This has to be done on board. They induce these chemicals into your system and change the chemical value of your body to match their chemical value. It heightens your telepathic ability and puts you on a terrific trip. You really start communicating freely, body-to-body, not mind-to-mind. In the hands of positive extraterrestrials it isn't dangerous. Type B negatives always have the tendency to over-do, and I do suppose they could blow you out. I don't think Type B uses it that much. I know Type C does use this fourth system.

The fifth system they use for communication is visual screening. This also has to be done on board. They don't try to communicate to you with sound. They transmit, in one form or another, images on a screen. You receive the pictures to understand what is going on. It is through the laser system that they can transmit your thought processes to pictures. I have seen it demonstrated, but I have never seen it used.

The two most efficient communication systems are the telepathic and the bio-chemical because they are both on the same wavelength. You simply flow information back and forth using the thought process.

Landing Procedures

I am now going to consider that a spacecraft has found its way into our star system and somehow decided it wanted to land on Planet Earth. If we are talking about major Mother Ships of the Type C and Type D, forget it. They won't land, but they will send man probes out. The same procedures apply to Type A ships. I do not know of any situation where a Type D ship has tried to land here within the last 25,000 years. The size of the ship, alone, would cause absolute panic. Where would you put it? It certainly would not land anyplace near people.

The following are landing procedures that *must* be followed by all space crafts in order to land:
1. They must locate the inner vortexual line of the planet because they have to come down that line when they start coming in for a landing. This is comparable to what we know today in aviation as the glide path at the airport that has to be followed. This is why we find ships coming into the same area all the time. For instance, there are more glide paths in New Mexico than, let's say, in Virginia.
2. They must maintain propulsion capability at seventy percent of readiness. The stories we hear about a ship touching down and immediately taking off was because the propulsion was never shut down. The propulsion system must be maintained at seventy percent of readiness at a second's notice. This is what makes the ship dangerous. There is radiation probability when you are getting near it.
3. They must have an adequate technical crew and *someone* on board who is technically capable of dealing with the atmosphere or the conditions of the landing site. If they had to send out a probe that does not have a trained technician, they will not land.

4. They must have a Mother Ship operating a probe directly. If they don't have a Mother Ship, they must have two probes operating in space to form a triangulation. This is a necessary safety device and is really important. Without a triangulation, you would have a good chance of the probe ship crashing or running into some other kind of trouble. For the most part, probe ships coming from Type C and Type D systems always come directly from a Mother Ship. By the way, Mother Ships are often hidden in clouds. If you know a Mother Ship is there, you can look at a cloud formation and it will be completely different than any other formation in the sky.
5. They must limit their time on the ground to a grelude formula. This is tricky, but I am going to give it to you because it is interesting. Who knows what might transpire in your life in the next few years.

Here is the grelude formula. If they touch down on earth, they limit their time to the time regression that is four percent of grelude ship size times twenty percent of total time out of their star base. The result of that formula is the maximum amount of time they can spend on the planet without running into a serious time regression problem that then affects consciousness.

Disease Regression

Extraterrestrials are also subject to what they call disease regression. By and large, they are not affected by our general virus problems. They are affected by the magnetic condition in our vortex. It is the magnetic vortex that they classify as a disease condition. The greatest danger is not getting sick, as we know it; the greatest danger is consciousness regression

Extraterrestrial Activities   61

that tends to diminish their consciousness capability. This means their ability to perform their functions on board is affected. To whatever extent they become incapacitated, they die.

If they stay on the planet longer than the amount of time limited in the grelude formula, they go into a highly accelerated state of disease regression. There is no backup on a ship. Everyone on board has a job, so if there is even one *individual* omitted they are in a lot of trouble. Consequently, if there are ten to fifteen members out on a probe and three of them go into a grelude time regression, there is probably no way they are going to get back to the Mother Ship because the probe does not have a built in time propulsion system like the Mother Ship does. If you have a small Type A, ten grelude ship, there is no way the ship would get back to star base in terms of the crew being alive because most of your Type A ships do not have a time limit system built into them. Only Type C and Type D ships have the built-in time limit systems. If a death were to occur for an extraterrestrial, consciousness would return to its star base system and operate the way it would normally operate if it were dead, whatever that may be.

Obviously, they are very careful about the time expended within the planet. After all, in most cases, the mission is just a probe mission or an evaluation mission, and they just get their stuff and get out. They take their readings for studying and measuring on those people they took on board. Then they throw them off and get out of there.

In the last fifty years, we have had mostly Type A ships; but I have high expectations that Type C ships will be here within the next few years. However, I don't know if they will make themselves known. I have had one Type D trip that was so overwhelming that I know I can gather all the valid information I need from Type C. I know my limits! Valid information is information that can be used in activity.

Spacecraft Encounters

Once again, valid information is information that can be used in activity. The following rules are of absolute necessity:
1. Do not be afraid, even Type B negatives do not intend to hurt you. Since most communication is telepathic, your fear is immediately transmitted. They do not pick it up as emotional fear, but they do pick it up as resistance. Emotions can cause some confusion in their operational mode.
2. If you have your wits about you, try to determine if the ship is of a grelude class or if it is a probe from a grelude. In most cases you won't see grelude ships because during the last fifty years, most of what is seen are probes. It is well for you to know what it is if you actually see one landing. There are not any Master Commanders on probes. You can know that if it is a probe, there is a Mother Ship someplace. You can tell immediately by its size if it is a grelude ship.
3. <u>Do not enter any probe ship</u>. In most cases, they don't have qualified facilities. You can observe occupants if they were to come out but make no move to enter a probe ship. That could be dangerous because they have no protective facilities for you. If it is a grelude ship, I wouldn't have much concern.
4. Don't even waste your time saying, "Hi there. My name is Frank." Immediately start dealing in telepathic thoughts. This means you have to be able to send and to listen.

5. Whether they are greludes or probes, when you are in communication, try to determine the type of mission the ship is on. This is done telepathically. If they know you know this, their reaction to you is going to be dramatically different, and you can get a lot of information. As a matter of fact, you might get all the rides you want.
6. Whether you go on board or not, remove all the metals from your body. That is probably one of the things that causes most negative reactions to a person's system. If you are invited on board, be sure to take off rings, necklaces, earrings, and belts. Leave them on the ground. You are undressed, anyway, when they do an investigation. Their system produces very strong electrical currents that are detrimental to us.
7. If you still have all your wits about you, ask for the Master Technician or The Agent. Don't stand there and have them lead you around. Stand in the doorway, remember your good manners, and express telepathically that you would like to have the opportunity to talk to the Master Technician or The Agent, <u>before you go on board</u>. Those are the two *individuals* who are most protective of your interests. In some cases, you would be taken to them anyway. It isn't the Master Commander that comes out.
8. Do not allow yourself to be used for measurement studies if at all possible. I am not suggesting you resist, rather let them know you are aware they are taking measurement studies, and you do not want to be used for that purpose. Indicate you will telepathically discuss with them anything they need to know that is within your purview to know.
9. Allow yourself to board a ship for touring purposes only. If you are invited on board, ask if they are going to take measurements, or if they want to show you around the ship.

Here is a scenario: A ship lands and I see it. It is close to me in proximity. The first thing I try to do is determine what type it is. I decide it is a Type C ship. I then know that it has some technicians on board and undoubtedly it has an Agent. I wait. A door opens and somebody gets out. We see each other, and I greet him telepathically. I indicate that I am on Planet Earth, and I have observed their landing. I ask the purpose of their mission. Are they probing? Are they here for an investigation? Are they taking measurements? I wait for an answer. They invite me on board. I say that I would like to talk to their Master Technician or to their Agent. They will understand this even though they don't use those terms. They bring forth a Master Technician or Agent and they invite me on board. I say that I would be happy to come on board providing it is understood that they are only going to give me a tour. I will discuss whatever it is they wish to discuss. However, I will not allow any measurements. If they agree to that, I am assured they won't break their word. If they don't agree to it, I don't go on board.

If it is a Type B, they want you on board right away, and they won't even have a discussion. They want to take measurements. If you communicate fear, they just pick you up and put you on board. If they know you are aware of what they are, Type B is especially less inclined to mishandle you. They would be more inclined to leave you alone and take off.

Debriefing

These are the rules I follow, even to this day, and even if the contact is very positive:
- Once you have made contact or have been on board and left, you must de-magnetize your

body immediately. Immerse yourself in water and then wrap both your wrists with copper wire. Tie the other end of the wire to a lead weight and put the weight on the ground for about one-half hour. The nervous system receives a tremendous amount of energy that you cannot handle. De-magnetization is the only way of doing it.

- Drink as much distilled water as you can hold.

- Put extra amounts of magnesium and iron into your system immediately.

- Take 15,000 milligrams of Pantothenic Acid because the adrenal glands are badly affected.

- Sit down and immediately write a report about the incident. Don't leave anything out. You were in a highly charged atmosphere in or around the ship, and it extremely important to discharge the energy in this way.

- Get a lot of rest and limit your activities for two or three days. I still do.

In the following Conclusion, macrocosmic and microcosmic principles expand upon our awareness that everything, including the extraterrestrial activities, has a function and is part of a natural progression. It is with this additional perspective that we come to better understand the Universal Laws and our individualized part in the Grand Design.

Conclusion
Macrocosmic & Microcosmic Principles

The further you go, the more extended you become.
---GT

You have heard the metaphysical phrase, "You are your own best physician. You know everything." You really do! It has been proven scientifically that there is a micro-millisecond before any event occurs that the brain knows what is about to occur. It has been proven in brain research that everyone knows the next move a millisecond before it happens. Since this is true, then you must already realize that the next logical sequence is that you know everything. Therefore, whatever problem you are faced with, you already know what the answer is going to be.

You may not be aware of the answer, but you already know what it is. What you are trying to do is logically find out, with awareness, what the answer is. You do this through the macrocosmic-microcosmic principles. The problem is committed to the macrocosm-you, but the answer is contained someplace in your microcosmic cells, not just between your ears. We can think just as well in our elbows, knees, or rear end as we do between our ears.

The brain is designed as a device to maintain a mechanical function. That's it! The thinking process is your whole body. When you go to little microcosmic cells inside your body, one of them (or a group of them) is going to have an answer for you. *BANG!* Just like that and it will come out of the blue. You will absolutely and completely know at which point you are finished with a problem. This is how I like to use the macrocosm-microcosmic principles.

The worse thing that has ever been perpetrated upon us is that we think up in our heads. When you allow yourself to become <u>micro</u>cosmic, and you go inside to the microcosmic cells, you have all the answers. You are not bereft of anything the Universe knows. Consequently, when an answer comes through (if it is true), you know it is true because there are all sorts of ways you can apply it. If an answer is not true, it can only be applied in one limited way and usually unsatisfactorily. Therefore, you know an answer by what it can do. A lie has no infinite possibilities of any results. It is truth that holds the infinite possibilities of results.

One cannot add to the one Universe. Therefore, you are always discovering (never inventing) the Universal Law that is always there. Let's take a relationship situation that may be of concern to you:
- Why are you in conflict?
- Is there any condition to harmonize that conflict?
- If there is a condition, is it worth harmonizing?

It may turn out that there isn't any need to harmonize the condition because it is a situation that is neither beneficial to you or to the other person. Or, it might be that you have something to deal with and the other person is dealing with something entirely different. The minute you have that awareness, you are half-way there because you know the direction you are headed. This is a self-inversion principle. You are looking inside of you. Therefore, you are not doing anything in violation to yourself or to another person. One of your consistent problems is that you don't look inside yourself and become your own microcosmic principle. Therefore, you really don't know what you are supposed to be doing because you don't know what the pulsation effect is inside of you. You are not paying attention. Listen inwardly to your heartbeat. That way you are coming close to the pulsation of the Universal principle.

I know this may sound silly, but let's take the example of drinking a glass of orange juice. Have you ever tried to follow the path of the orange juice to discover what is going on inside the cells? The minute you do this, you begin to have a great affinity with yourself. At that point, you become aware of the great range of your cellular functions that are a part of you. After all, if your stomach is upset, you are not going to feel well. An upset stomach destroys your whole attitude. You need to know that you are harmonizing with the close relationship you have to your internal workings.

The closer you get to what is going on microcosmically inside of you, the more harmonious you become. An individual can be in irritation to his own flow, but if he were harmoniously aware and practiced the microcosmic principle on his own, he wouldn't have the irritation of disease from the very beginning. What is microcosmic principle? We will be discussing that as we go along.

You will never run out of things to learn on this plane and whatever pursuits you explore hereafter. Never! You can pursue, and pursue, and pursue, and you will never reach the ultimate. You just go on and on expanding upon all your knowledge and experience. I think that is the most exciting thing in the world! If you couldn't go on to learn everything, there wouldn't be any sense to learn anything. You could just sit and do nothing if there were an end point. I don't ever want to sit and do nothing. The macrocosmic and microcosmic principles wouldn't allow for that, anyway.

I also don't care what you have been told, read, or believe; the Universe cannot be aware of any part of itself, or It would become finite and that would destroy Its infinity. Knowing It is complete, It has nothing else to do to Itself. Maintenance is not an issue to perfection, and the Universe *is* at the point of perfection. It doesn't have to look out and say, "Oh, look, that planet is out of control. We have to do something." It doesn't have to say that tomorrow *We* are going to make a new solar system because *We* have this space out here, and *We* have to put something in it. It doesn't do this because It has no awareness.

All the Universe knows is that whatever is complete is the principle behind It, and the complete principle behind It is infinity. That is why we will never know what the complete principle is in totality.

There are macrocosmic characteristics I would like to share with you. I will then follow these with elements that are characteristic of the microcosm.

Macrocosmic Characteristics

The first characteristic of macrocosmic principle: It is complete wherever you go. Nothing can be added to it or taken away from it. It is complete unto itself.

The second characteristic of the macrocosmic principle: It is the ultimate level of self-sufficiency. It does not need or want *anything* in order to exist. Left alone the macrocosm will do everything necessary. Its power level never changes. If you have a problem and the solution does not appear in three minutes, drop the problem. The answer will come in another way. Humans *think* problems and divorce themselves from the macrocosmic principle.

The third characteristic of the macrocosmic principle: It is infinite. The reason it does not have a beginning or an end point is because it cannot run out of completeness. We struggle with development because we forget infinitude.

Why do little things that prove nothing? Take giant steps! The minute you find something good, go to the next better thing. Everything is designed to be a springboard to the next better thing. Did you ever stop to realize that you are the end terminal point of eight and one-half billion years of evolution on Planet Earth? How good is that!

The fourth characteristic of the macrocosmic principle: Macrocosm moves on an invert-extrovert action pattern. Action allows it to be infinite. The life energy moves in and out and turns in and out upon itself like a wave action that never repeats itself. The elements from the Universe wash in and wash out, and we are in the midst of the sea. Another way to look at this is like the flowing action of kneading dough. If you put a drop of red dye into bread dough when you are kneading dough, you can see the pattern never repeats itself. Cycles roll. Movement makes a vortex. Just as electricity doesn't run in a straight line, macrocosm does not know a straight-line motion. If we insist on straight-line movement in our lives, we are in opposition to this principle. The shortest distance between two points is introversion-extroversion action. It is pulsation that moves you in a direction, not straight-line movement.

Be aware of the two elements when you breathe in (introversion) and breathe out (extroversion). Using this same principle, the flow principle itself moves you. Then there is no resistance. The flow goes on and on and on, and you have the ebb and flow of that feeling. Use your whole body unit as the Universal macrocosm with billions of microcosmic units (cells) within it. Use your cells. Your cells are all working within a macrocosmic unit that you call you. In principle, you know everything because you are an integral particle of the Universe. Work to produce what you want to produce and stop using your mind as a macrocosm in your life. Straight-line lives are against the character of energy flow.

It may surprise you that the <u>macro</u>cosmic characteristics do not transfer into the <u>micro</u>cosmic areas. The macrocosm and microcosm do not have the same characteristics. Here is where the would-be occult writer can throw you way off. The writer would lead you to believe that to outline the macrocosmic characteristics immediately assumes that all the elements of the macrocosm are true in the microcosm. This is absolutely not true.

Here are the characteristics of the microcosm.

<u>Micro</u>cosmic Characteristics

<u>The first characteristic of the microcosmic principle</u>: It is aware of a finite point of the macrocosm. As already stated, the macrocosm isn't aware of anything. This does not mean a characteristic of the microcosm has a beginning and ending point, per se. However, it does have a beginning and ending in so far that it knows itself at any given point. What is the microcosm? It is you. Just the fact that you know you are sitting reading at this given point and time (indicated by a human clock and calendar) makes you finite to the degree of your awareness. You know that surrounding you is the macrocosm condition that is the Universe. You might not be terribly aware of it, but you are basically aware of it.

What makes you a microcosm is the fact you have developed awareness of a given point. 'Aware' is not even within the realm of macrocosm. In other words, and once again, the Universe isn't aware of itself. It just is, and It knows It is, but It isn't aware that It is. It cannot be aware of a single point.

It is the microcosmic principle that lets you know where you are. We have to have finite points and to be able to establish points A-B-C-D in the microcosm. If I want to go from point

A to point B, I move a certain way. The principle of the macrocosm doesn't go along with that movement to that degree. That does not make this a negative situation. It is a microcosmic characteristic that allows you to accomplish, because microcosm points out to you when you have come up against a negative. Microcosm also points out where you can become more harmonious with the macrocosmic principle. I have never been anywhere astrally in the Universe where I can honestly say that consciousness was not aware of a finite point. In other words, everything is microcosmic within the macrocosm.

Wherever you go and in whatever galaxy, you will always find a point of awareness along the way. The microcosmic principle follows wherever you go. Awareness is essential, because if we did not have a point of awareness, we would not have the ability to design a learning system. What would happen if I could wave a magic wand and say, "Zap, from this moment on you are all macrocosmic"? You would all be in oblivion because you wouldn't be aware of anything. In effect, you would be wiped out. For millions of years, mystics and wise men have been trying to tell us that individuals are operating as a microcosmic principle attuned to the macrocosmic principle when seen through this light.

The second characteristic of microcosmic principle: Microcosmic infinity is in its incompleteness and that is its infinity. Its incompleteness keeps it infinite because no matter what you think, you are never satisfied. That is your infinity. If money is all you want in life, and I supply you with all that money, you will find something else you want. I have had my share of people with a holier-than-thou attitude tell me, "I need nothing. I feel fine. I am perfect. God loves me" and off they go. I look at them and think that we might as well put them in a cage and lock them in. That is ridiculous.

You always have to be in a state of being unfilled, or you couldn't go on learning. You have got to have the 'wants'. You need the situation of wanting because it is the thing that keeps pointing you to finite awareness. The situation of wanting is the necessary progression for the fulfillment of the microcosmic principle. People who don't have a sense of incompleteness are losing both the microcosmic and the macrocosmic principles.

It is those who go in a straight line to work, come home, watch TV, and go to bed who get very little out of life. They are very unhappy people. No matter how they appear on the outside, they are not happy internally because they have very little connection to the microcosmic principle of incompleteness. You always have to look for something else. Obviously, you can make this a ridiculous point and carry it to extremes.

The third characteristic of the microcosmic principle: It is sufficient only to the degree of its awareness. The key word here is sufficient. In other words, the microcosmic principle can be insufficient. This applies to the person who runs a straight-line life because they are not aware of where they are. Therefore, they are not aware of where they can go. In order to have the microcosmic principle operate, it must be sufficient in relationship to its degree of awareness. If you see yourself as nowhere and going nowhere, you aren't even in a microcosmic sense. You haven't fulfilled anything. In the microcosmic principle, you have always got to have some identification to know where you are. That is absolutely essential. You have to know where you stand so you know where you can go. You need to know your efficiencies and your deficiencies.

The fourth characteristic of the microcosmic principle: It is the inverse energy of flow or motion. Everything that comes to it immediately moves inside and does not come out again. The microcosmic energy is the inverse fuel inside the engine that moves us to another point of awareness. If we had energy come in and had it flow out, we would be doing exactly what the macrocosm is doing. We would just be there. We wouldn't be doing anything. Under this consideration, we are not macrocosmic, we are microcosmic. Consequently, we take all the energy in (we take all the experience in) on an inverse flow, and when the energy reaches a particular point, we move to another point of awareness and experience. We are free to move (whether it is a physical, mental or spiritual motion) by taking in another flow of energy that moves us to another point where we expend the energy again. We don't expend it outward. We expend the energy <u>in the awareness and in the knowledge</u>. It is the expenditure of awareness that gives you another view.

Reminder: The <u>macro</u>cosm is a complete principle that cannot be added to because it is self-sufficient. Consequently, you cannot add anything to a complete Universe. What you actually do is to take energy in on an inverse principle that moves you to another part of the experience. A move expends the energy, and you take the energy in again. Obviously, this is happening every second. By thinking about something, you are absorbing the energy (using it up). Using the energy is why the energy doesn't blow up by compression. Anything you know makes you a better individual, even the things you know you don't like. Every experience adds to your character of energy, and the character of energy is that it doesn't take up any space. No matter how much you use, you don't change the character of energy at all. You can have billions and billions of years of experience and your energy of awareness never puts on one ounce of weight, nor does it grow one inch taller.

The fifth characteristic of the microcosmic principle: In finality, microcosm always responds to the macrocosm. This completes the circle. No matter what experience you have, no matter how good, bad, or indifferent you are; and no matter under what conditions you run your life, you will eventually and inexorably respond to the macrocosmic principle. No matter how you slice the cake, you are still unequivocally (without any doubt whatsoever) always responding to the macrocosmic principle. No matter how you look at it, you are the master of your own ship; but you do not really rule life. The macrocosmic principle rules the life in which you partake. At the moment you die, your response is pretty much on a Universal level.

Let's review the five microcosmic characteristics:

- First characteristic of the microcosmic principle:
  It is aware of a finite point of the macrocosm.

- Second characteristic of the microcosmic principle:
  Its infinity is in its finitude.

- Third characteristic of the microcosmic principle:
  It is sufficient only to the degree of its awareness.

- Fourth characteristic of the microcosmic principle:
  It moves only on its inverse action, expanding its energy as it moves from one experience to another.

- Fifth characteristic of the microcosmic principle:
  In finality, microcosm always responds to the macrocosmic principle.

Since I am giving you this knowledge based on the principles of microcosm and macrocosm, the smartest thing for me to do is to use the Universe as a macrocosm and myself as the microcosm. This is true because of the kind of material we are dealing with and for what I am trying to get across to you. On the other hand, when I am dealing with a business arrangement, I don't need all that energy from the Universe. I can go to myself as the <u>macro</u>cosmic principle and use my cells as the <u>micro</u>cosmic principle. The answers are always there and very close to me.

You see, once you understand the characteristics of the macrocosmic principle, you don't have to go way out in the Universe to apply it. You can start with your thought process and your application of the principle at any elementary level you wish. You can partake of the macrocosmic principle to whatever degree you are willing to be aware of your experience. The only thing you must be careful *not to do* is to confuse the macrocosmic principle with microcosmic principle. It is fine if you are going to look at your body as a macrocosm; but you have to realize that when you begin to look at the microcosm, you don't just have a mind operating the body. No! No! No!

Macrocosm can really be anything you want it to be. We have been talking about it in terms of the Universe; but the macrocosmic principle can be applied to the Universe or to a galaxy, a solar system, a planet, to a mass of people, or even to an individual. <u>Here is where we lose the basic knowledge that is so very essential.</u> Because I deal in this kind of work, I certainly would prefer to think of the macrocosm on a Universal level. It gives me this tremendously infinite playground to go out and do things. However, when you start thinking about this world, you can also look at the world as a macrocosm. There are enough microcosmic elements to the world to make the world a macrocosm and the elements the microcosm.

In fact, why not think of your body as a macrocosm? How

many cells do you have inside your body? Within your body there are a few trillion cells joined together in an activity as a macrocosm. You can look at your hand with hundreds of thousand of little elements that are contained within that macrocosmic thing you call a hand. If you want to look at your whole body as the macrocosm, you have to look at the cellular function inside the body made up of those trillions of cells as the microcosmic principle of macrocosm body.

If and when you choose to use your body as the macrocosm, then use all of your cells as the microcosm. All of a sudden, you will discover huge things about yourself that you have never discovered before because you took them for granted. You won't take your heart and lungs for granted anymore when you start thinking about the cells as microcosmic principles inside the macrocosmic body. You become aware of pieces of cellular microcosmic functions doing their *thing*. You find yourself expanding from the microcosm into the macrocosm when you think about your five toes as extremities on your foot, or what your eyes are doing, what your liver is doing to purify, or what your spleen is doing. Think about all the elements involved. However, you must always remember where the line is between macrocosm principle and microcosmic principle. Do not take microcosm as if it were macrocosm.

The minute you start thinking of yourself as macrocosm, you have to think in macrocosmic terms. This is where we fall down. In our own use of this principle (where it can do the most good), we fall down because we are so use to thinking of ourselves as little microcosmic beings in terms of the world around us and to the Universe we live in as macrocosmic. However, when you sit down to think about *you,* keep the macrocosmic principle. What most people do is to divorce themselves. Literally, they cut themselves off from the higher macrocosm, and they don't think about it anymore. This is why you can't solve problems. You don't go inside yourself microcosmically to consider yourself as a macrocosm.

Give some thought to this principle. It works this way: If I use any element out in the Universe that I can identify, I am working on a microcosm-to-microcosm basis. That is because I can identify an element that becomes finite by identification. We can define the element any place we want to put it.

When I only think about the Universe as macrocosm, I can't identify anything. All I can see is this little microcosmic me inside this enormously huge thing (the Universe) with all these principles that I can be aware of. When I sit down with a standard religious person and say, "Out there someplace is God," I am immediately using finite terms. I have taken the eraser, and I have wiped out macrocosmic principle. I am looking at another microcosm. Two microcosms can't help each other because they have no macrocosm to hold onto. They are just staring at each other. One of us (me) says, "God, will you help me?" and God says, "No, I can't because I am not big enough to help you. I am no bigger than you are." You say, "Where is the help going to come from?" God answers, "I don't know." This conversation could go on like this forever until I stop and say, "Enough of this!"

This is why the concept of man and God will never work. The reason that concept will never work is that when man is thinking in terms of his problems and himself, he immediately divorces himself from the macrocosmic principle. 'God' is not a satisfactory macrocosmic principle primarily because God has always been known (and used in our modern times) as some singular, finite identifiable point named 'God'. What you have is two microcosmic points trying to look at each other. They have nothing bigger to hold onto. When you can face God with you as the macrocosm and then think of yourself microcosmically with a few billion cells working to produce whatever it is you want to produce, you will *always* come out of it beautifully. You will never really be lost.

I have an identifiable me (five-foot and so may odd inches tall, so much weight, and so much length in my arms) ah, there is my macrocosmic consciousness. I stop using my mind as a microcosm and say, "I have a few billion cells here all of them microcosmic. " Now, I can do anything with *me*. I am setting me as an identifiable body unit in the same category as Universal macrocosm. At that point, I am in the flow and being needed in just the way I should be needed. I am looking at myself in the only way I can look at myself and still be in line with the principle microcosmically.... not as one-unit person but as billions of little microscopic things going on. The cells in my toes are helping me, the cells in my intestines are helping me, and the cells in my brain are all helping me. They are all working according to the microcosmic principle. This is the biggest thing you could ever do.

Never try to think out a problem unless you can be completely relaxed and be alone. Seriously. Never try when you are in a hubbub of activity or under any kind of time pressure. Make the ideal circumstances for yourself. For a lot of reasons, the best place in the world to work out a problem is in a hot tub of water. Get alone and get comfortable. The situation has already been identified by you. In effect, you have already programmed it into your consciousness. You really don't have to define it any further, although make sure the situation is clear and not fuzzy. At this particular point, leave it alone because it has been programmed macrocosmically. Stop thinking of yourself as an individual human being and start inverting your thoughts to all of your cells.

As I have already said, leave the problem alone. Think of all these billions of little micro-functions that are going on inside of your ears, your eyes, your heart, and any other area of your body that you wish to access. Now, the more you think of these parts of you and expand from your toes on up to the top of your head, the more aware you become, the more you are expanding. The answer to the 'problem' will come right up to you as part of your awareness. You don't even have to think about it.

We constantly feel we are faced with insolvable problems. That is not *ever* true. Put your focus upon you. Just remember that when a problem is left, it is left in the macrocosm that is your total being. You then work from little microscopic points putting the focus on you. This principle allows you to know yourself as an integral part of the Universe. This principle allows you to know yourself as exactly what you are!

You are not going to take a jackhammer to drive a tack into the wall without knocking down the whole wall. It doesn't need that much pressure. In that same sense, we like to feel we can call upon the Universe to solve our problems. We don't *need* that much energy to solve our problems. We are faced with a lot of minor problems, not major ones. Our problems are really relatively small. Be efficient. Efficiency, as we are using it here, provides you with the ability to use macrocosmic-microcosmic principles to solve problems within yourself.

Keep this simple. Everything on Planet Earth is subject to man's dominion. It is a basic Genesis principle that we have been given dominion, and that includes the relationship of man and his dominion to himself and to his consciousness. The closer you become microcosmically to the macrocosm, the more harmonious you are going to find yourself, your life, and the whole totality of your experience. Once you learn this, you can use it wherever you go.

From The Collected Works of Gregge Tiffen

Life in the World Hereafter: The Journey Continues

Life in the World Hereafter Journal

First Encounter Series:
  No. 1 Into the Universe: Extraterrestrial Activities
  No. 2 Down to Earth: Terrestrial Activities
  No. 3 Earth and Second Earth

Questions and More Questions

2010 Booklet of the Month Series:
  The Journey Continues

2009 Booklet of the Month Series:
  The Language of a Mystic

2008 Booklet of the Month Series:
  Lessons in Living

2007 Booklet of the Month Series:
  Seasonal Reflections

2006 Thanksgiving: The Power of Prayer
2006 Winter Solstice: The Christmas Story

All publications are available
directly from P Systems
P.O. Box 12754
La Jolla, CA 92039

For Credit card orders and detailed descriptions visit:
www.P-SystemsInc.com/publications
For bulk orders call toll free: 1.888.658.0668

www.ingramcontent.com/pod-product-compliance
Lightning Source LLC
LaVergne TN
LVHW011732060526
838200LV00051B/3160